About the Author

Duncan Bannatyne is one of Britain's best-known entrepreneurs thanks to his appearances on *Dragons' Den*. A regular investor in new companies, he is chairman of the Bannatyne Group, which owns and operates hotels, health clubs, spas and bars. In 2010, the *Sunday Times* Rich List estimated his personal worth at £320 million, having started his business career with an investment of £450 in an ice-cream van.

His first book, *Anyone Can Do It*, was a *Sunday Times* bestseller in both hardback and paperback and has sold in excess of 200,000 copies. He has six children, and homes in London, the North East of England and the south of France.

Duncan's blog can be found at www.bannatyne.co.uk or you can follow him on Twitter at twitter.com/duncanbannatyne

Jo Monroe, who has worked with Duncan Bannatyne on all his books, is a ghostwriter and journalist who has written for *The Times*, the *Guardian* and *Time Out*.

Her website is www.jomonroe.com

DUNCAN BANNATYNE

43

Mistakes Businesses Make

...and how to avoid them

headline

business plus

First published in 2011
by HEADLINE PUBLISHING GROUP

1

Cataloguing in Publication Data is available from the British Library

ISBN 978 0 7553 6226 4

Typeset in Stone Serif by Avon DataSet Ltd,
Bidford-on-Avon, Warwickshire

Printed and bound in Great Britain by
Clays Ltd, St Ives, Suffolk

Headline's policy is to use papers that are natural, renewable and recyclable products and made from wood grown in sustainable forests. The logging and manufacturing processes are expected to conform to the environmental regulations of the country of origin.

HEADLINE PUBLISHING GROUP
An Hachette UK Company
338 Euston Road
London NW1 3BH

www.headline.co.uk
www.hachette.co.uk

TO MY CHILDREN

Abigail, Hollie, Jennifer, Eve, Emily and Tom.
Remember I love you more . . .

Acknowledgements

First and foremost I would like to thank my beautiful wife Joanne, and my children, Abigail, Hollie, Jennifer, Eve, Emily, Tom and not forgetting my grandchild Ava. Thank you and I love you all so much.

I would like to thank Jo Monroe for working with me for a fifth time; it has been an absolute pleasure. My thanks are also due to Chris Barnardo and Richard Blakesley from The Wand Company for their input on obtaining patents. Thanks also to John Moseley at Headline Publishing and Jonny Geller at Curtis Brown; your help with this book has been invaluable.

A big thank you to everyone.

Contents

Introduction

On the face of it, a book about the biggest mistakes in business might sound a bit negative. But knowing where other ventures have failed and avoiding the same mistakes yourself is a positive way of making sure your business becomes a success.

The inspiration for this book comes from the nine series of *Dragons' Den* I have taken part in. Series after series, year after year, businesses fail to get investment in the Den – and then subsequently fail altogether – because they make the same mistakes some businesses have always made. I'm not talking about the insignificant things, like not wearing a suit for a presentation or momentarily getting your figures wrong, I'm talking about those fundamental flaws that – once identified – mean a business can never succeed. Insufficient revenue, an unidentified rival, a lack of appetite for the product by consumers: these are the flaws we encounter on every day of filming, and there have been times when I've sat there and thought: 'Does someone really think this is a *business*?'

A business is not just a good idea, it is a venture that produces revenue at such a level that it makes a profit. The Dragons have seen hundreds of good ideas that turned out to be poor businesses, and hundreds of ventures that could create revenue, but not at sufficiently high levels to exceed their costs. We have also, it has to be said, seen some really, *truly* dumb ideas! In this book, I've pulled together the most common reasons why businesses fail to attract investment, customers and revenues.

If you know where the pitfalls are, then you will be able to avoid them and make sure you won't repeat the errors others have made in the past. Some of the mistakes in this book are so obvious that they're laughable, while others are cunning and hidden and will snatch your business from your grasp when you're least expecting it. I'll also tell you why I think some of the biggest business failures in recent years happened: I still find it shocking that a name a big as Woolworths has disappeared from our high streets. And if it can happen to Woolworths, it can happen to anyone.

When some people talk about business failures, they mention high-profile cases like Enron's collapse or the Bernie Madoff scandal. To my mind, those businesses didn't make mistakes, they committed crimes and for that reason they have no place in this book. What does have a place here, however, is the mistake Madoff's clients made when they invested with him: they failed to do their research and made an unwise choice. This isn't a book about fraud and corporate crimes, it's a book about the oversights, errors of judgement and omissions that we are all capable of making if we fail to pay attention. The billion-pound collapses might steal the headlines, but it is the tiniest error that can steal your business from under you if you're not clued up.

Duncan Bannatyne
March 2011

MISTAKE 1

Not taking good advice

ONLY A SMALL PERCENTAGE OF PEOPLE WHO APPEAR ON *Dragons' Den* get investment, but absolutely everyone goes away with valuable advice. Between the five Dragons, there aren't many business models we haven't tried or situations we haven't been in. We're a pretty good bunch to ask for advice.

> *Getting advice in business isn't hard, but getting good advice is.*

Getting advice in business isn't hard, but getting *good* advice is. Everyone, from your customers and your suppliers to your staff – not to mention friends and family – are all very good at pointing out where you're going wrong. The problem is that very few people will tell you how to put things right. And the people who do make suggestions are very often the bankers, lawyers and accountants who stand to make more money from you if you do what they say.

This perhaps explains why entrepreneurs get used to ignoring advice. They tell themselves that no one knows their business as well as they do, that no one has their vision for the company and that everyone is after a piece of their success. The result is that good counsel is disregarded along with all the rubbish suggestions.

Early on in my career I didn't have anyone I could ask for advice. No one in my family had started a business – my father even told me that 'people like us don't start businesses' – and my friends were all employees, or unemployed. Because I had to figure things out the hard way, I probably put a higher value on good advice than most entrepreneurs. I always urge first–time entrepreneurs to find themselves a mentor; someone who has made a success of their business, or of several businesses, who can be at the end of the phone when things get tough. There's nothing like having someone you trust pointing out shortcomings and oversights.

However, most of us find asking for help and advice difficult, which probably explains why so many people would rather pick up a book like this than pick up the phone and call someone who could help. We feel we should be able to work things out on our own. What you find out with experience is that asking for advice is actually a hell of a lot easier than acting on it. Even when you hear something that you know makes sense, there's a tendency to say, 'I'll do that tomorrow,'

2

or 'I'll do that if nothing else works.' That's because good advice is rarely easy advice to take.

There wasn't anyone around to tell me when I was making a mistake and it's my hope that this book will stop you from stumbling into some of the hurdles that tripped me up. You won't like everything I've got to say, but one of the hardest lessons I've learned along the way was that the advice you don't want to hear is probably the advice you should listen to the most!

MISTAKE 2

Failure to take responsibility

PEOPLE OFTEN TALK ABOUT THEIR BUSINESSES AS IF THEY'RE children and I completely understand why. You love your business, you nurture it, you worry about it and you have hopes and ambitions for it. But what some people forget is that, like your children, you must also take responsibility for your business.

If there is one single over-riding reason why businesses fail it is because the person or people in charge of them think that someone else will sort out their problems. There have been many times when entrepreneurs have come into the Den asking for investment that they didn't really need: either their cashflow was sufficient or they had access to funds elsewhere. What they really wanted wasn't the Dragons' money; they wanted a Dragon to take care of things. They wanted someone to step into their business and straighten out their accounts, improve their systems or make the difficult phone calls. To put it simply: they wanted someone else to take responsibility.

I've spent over 30 years in business, and I lost count a long time ago of the number of times I heard someone complaining their business was in trouble because of a client. And if it wasn't a client, it was an employee. Or a supplier. Or the market. Or the economy. Or a rival. I can count on one hand the number of people who have admitted to me that their business failed because they weren't up to the job.

> 66 Let me make it clear: you are responsible for everything your business does. 99

If you have a difficult client, you need to ask why you are still dealing with them. If you have a troublesome employee, you need to examine your recruitment process and your disciplinary procedure to see why you hired them in the first place and if they've been poorly managed. If your suppliers are overcharging or underperforming, then you should already know the names of two other suppliers you could use instead. If the market has changed, why hasn't your business responded to that change? If a rival is hammering your profits, what should you be learning from them? All businesses face hurdles and obstacles. It is how we tackle them that shapes our success.

If you think I'm being unduly hard, then I'd question if you're tough enough to succeed in business. People often think that success in business comes from being ruthless, but I don't think that's true: in my experience success in business comes from being tough. Tough enough to do the dirty jobs and tough enough to make the difficult decisions.

What happens when lines of responsibility become blurred

In 2010, the world was given a very stark reminder of what happens when people in business fail to take responsibility for their actions. In my opinion, the oil spill in the Gulf of Mexico was a classic case of shirked responsibility. The construction of the Deepwater Horizon well that exploded on 20 April 2010 with the loss of eleven lives had been carried out by one company. I'll call it Company A. The rig was owned by Company B. The construction of the well that would feed the rig with oil was being built by Company C. Which of these companies do you think was BP? None of them. BP was Company D, which held a temporary lease on the rig. With so many companies involved, it's perhaps not surprising that each party initially thought responsibility for the accident lay with one of the other companies. And once thousands of gallons of oil a day were spilling into the ocean, the issue of responsibility was further clouded – was it the state of Louisiana that was responsible for coordinating the clean-up? Or the federal government in the US? Or the Department of Energy?

With so many companies involved in the oil spill, and with so many different agencies involved in its regulation and clean-up, it doesn't seem all that surprising to me that a) the spill happened in the first place; and b) it took so long to get the spill under control. No one knew who was responsible for what or who was ultimately in charge.

You might be wondering what one of the biggest corporate disasters in history has got to do with your business. Let me tell you: everything. It is a warning to everyone who delegates responsibility for vital tasks to employees or outsources work to third-party agencies. Although you might not be physically doing the work yourself, you are still responsible for it being done to the right standard and by the right deadline.

In my own case, I would never outsource something like the cleaning of my health clubs, for example. Other operators invite cleaning companies to bid for the contract to clean their clubs, thereby passing on the responsibility of hiring staff, drawing up rosters and organising payroll for them to the contractor. In my clubs, we have our cleaners on our payroll. If one of my health club managers thinks something hasn't been cleaned properly, he or she can take immediate action because the cleaner is a member of staff. In other operators' clubs the cleaners don't report to the manager, they report to their boss at the cleaning agency. I've found that as soon as the line of responsibility becomes blurred, there is room for error.

My business interests will never be as complicated or as big as an oil company, but they are growing every year, and that means every year my responsibilities increase. In my first business – operating an ice-cream van – I did everything from the van maintenance to buying cornets and wafers at the wholesalers to selling the ice cream and defrosting the freezers. In one-man-band businesses it's pretty obvious who is responsible for everything, but my view didn't change when the business grew. When I had several employees, I still considered myself responsible for everything they did. I might no longer have been the one selling the ice creams or cleaning the freezers, but it was my fault if sales dropped off or the freezers weren't clean enough for the health and safety inspector. I felt that it was my responsibility to make sure that I had hired the right people and trained them in the right way.

The bucks stops with me.

These days, even though I now have thousands of employees, I still feel exactly the same way. From the rate of interest the business pays on its loans to the menu in our cafes, everything that happens in a Bannatyne's health club or in one of our hotels is ultimately down to me. If there are insufficient staff on duty, if the changing rooms haven't been cleaned properly or if the Zumba classes are overbooked it's ultimately my fault because I didn't create the right management structure, I didn't train my staff properly or I didn't anticipate the increased interest in Zumba. In each of my clubs, I have a poster with my email address on it and I invite our members to get in touch if they're not happy with anything. The buck still stops with me.

DIY: Do-It-Yourself

Shirking responsibility is particularly tempting if you are new to business. Of course your bank manager knows more about finance than you do, so naturally you would defer to them. And your accountants know more about payroll or VAT than you do, so it's only natural that you would do what they suggest. And probably a lot of the people you hire will have expertise that exceeds your own as they will be specialists in sales, marketing, cookery, aerobics or whatever else your business requires. New entrepreneurs are very vulnerable to thinking their expertise and knowledge is worth less than those of the people they surround themselves with.

Entrepreneurs can be very tight about giving away equity in their business, but giving away so much emotional equity in their venture is a far more damaging way to dilute their investment. If you start to think that the business isn't wholly yours, it becomes easier to let the little things slide.

If you're new to business, I urge you to do your own accounts, sort out your own VAT and make the sales calls yourself. The more you know your business, the more you can take responsibility for it. The more responsibility you take, the more you will understand your business and the more able you will be to delegate the right tasks to the right people as the business grows. After all, how can you successfully employ an accountant or a general manager if you don't know what their job involves? I don't think I'd be as successful running a big business now if I hadn't once been responsible for every single aspect of a much smaller business.

MISTAKE 3

Not understanding the difference between a good idea and a good business

MANY PEOPLE HAVE HAD THAT THRILLING MOMENT DOWN the pub where they come up with their Big Idea. A group of friends ask the barman for a pen and begin to write down their million-pound sure-fire hit on a beer mat. Before long, they've gone off and started their business full of enthusiasm and hope, but then, a few months later, they are back in the pub arguing about whose stupid idea it was. And probably whose round it is.

There are lots of reasons why good ideas don't make good businesses. It's a really nice idea, for instance, to buy cheap property, renovate it and sell it for a profit. There have been countless TV shows based on just that premise, yet lots of people have lost a lot of money doing that because a) cheap property is either hard to find or cheap for a reason, b) renovations always cost more than you think they will, and c) you end up needing to sell for too high a price and you can't get a buyer to bite.

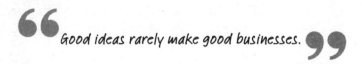

It might be a nice *idea* to turn your hobby of flower arranging into a business, but how many people actually pay for flower arranging? It might be a really great *idea* to open a pub, but if you're tied into supply deals with breweries that mean you can't compete with your rivals, you might not have any customers. Good ideas don't always – in fact they rarely – make good businesses.

But new ideas, especially Big Ideas, are very exciting and they seem to possess some kind of magic power that blinds people to common sense. People get so caught up in their new idea, and become so full of enthusiasm and passion for it, that they never stop to ask if their good idea has any hope of becoming a good business.

So how can you tell if your idea stands a chance of becoming a business? You can start by coming up with serious answers to the following five questions:

1. Why isn't anyone else doing it?

Usually, there's a bloody good reason why and if you can figure it out you can save yourself a lot of pain.

2. Who will buy your product or service?

If the answer is either 'I would' or 'My mum says she would' then alarm bells should start ringing. Obviously starting a business with two customers is better than none, but if you can't instantly think of the kinds of people who will buy your product or service, then come up with another idea.

3. How many of those people are there?

Some businesses – like corner shops – need hundreds of customers or clients a day, others – like luxury yacht builders – only need one or two a year. How many customers would your business need? And realistically, how many of those potential customers would use your service ahead of an existing one? If you have premises, how far will people travel to buy from you? In my own business, we have estimated that the most people will drive to use a gym is ten minutes. How big is your catchment area?

4. How much would those people be willing to pay?

What is the real benefit of your idea? If it only marginally improves people's lives or is only marginally more convenient or slightly better than existing provision, the chances are that your potential customers won't take the risk of trying out your offering and they'll stick with what they know. So you need to ask yourself how likely it is that people will select and pay you for your product or service. If you had to put a price on how much someone would take out of their own pocket and hand over to you, what would that price realistically be? Not enough? Go back to the beer mat and try again. Finally, multiply your number of potential customers by the amount you think they will realistically pay: this is your turnover.

5. What will your costs be?

You won't be able to anticipate every cost you'll incur in your business, but while you're sitting around in the pub you can probably have a pretty decent stab at coming up with a figure. When I opened my first residential care home in the mid-1980s, I didn't know what all my costs would be, but I managed to estimate them fairly accurately. For instance, the government stipulated the staff:resident ratio, and the salary I had to pay could be found in recruitment ads. I guessed the likely size of utility bills by multiplying my household bills by nine because the care home was nine times bigger than my house. You won't be able to think of everything, but a sober guesstimate should get you to a plausible figure. Now deduct that figure from your turnover: this is your profit.

Take a long hard look at that profit figure. Is that enough for you to live on? Will you have to share that profit with the other people in the pub? Don't forget you'll have to pay tax on your profit.

Only you can decide if that figure constitutes a 'good business'. Some people are very happy to run relatively small businesses, others – like me – want the thrill of building big businesses with big profits. A good business for you might not be a good business for me, and vice versa. But if you're happy with your profit potential, then congratulations: your good idea has the potential to be a good business.

MISTAKE 4

It's just a bad idea

STARTING A NEW BUSINESS BASED ON A GOOD IDEA IS hard enough. Starting with a bad idea? You'd have to be a masochist.

One of the reasons *Dragons' Den* is so popular – and why it's such fun to make – is because every now and then someone comes into the Den with a truly terrible idea. It can be very hard not to seem cruel when entrepreneurs tell us they've spent six-figure sums and left their jobs to start these businesses, but it is our job to tell them to stop spending, stop trying and stop dreaming.

In my opinion, one of the worst ideas we've seen has got to be what became known as 'the cucumber condom', a plastic device you stick on the end of a cucumber to stop it drying out. As the inventor of Q-Top went through his pitch I found so many flaws that I didn't really know where to begin with my questions. While I imagine a couple of people watching probably did say to the person next to them on the sofa: 'That's quite a good idea,' I am certain that the majority of people watching were saying, 'Why don't you just cut the end off the cucumber?'

What need does your business fulfil?

The reason why I thought Q-Top was a bad idea wasn't that the ends of cucumbers don't dry out, it was that the drying out of cucumbers isn't really a problem for anyone. And why would you fiddle around with the Q-Top when it's much easier to discard the dry first slice? Even if you were given your Q-Top for free you probably wouldn't use it.

Q-Top is one of the Den's howlers because it attempted to solve a problem that no one was aware they had. And you can't build a business for those two people watching who thought it was *quite* a good idea. Businesses need *bloody* good ideas to thrive.

In the first series, an entrepreneur called Mark Greenhalgh brought us Cabtivate, a business that offered video advertising in the back of black cabs. The idea was to sell the video equipment to cabbies for hundreds of pounds, and in return give them a share of the advertising revenue. The trouble as I saw it was that it would take so long for the cabbies to get their investment back that they were better off sticking with the paper ads they already had – especially as passengers would ask them to turn the TV off so they could have a conversation! However, that's only my opinion and I gather Cabtivate did get off the ground.

Other notable Den duds include an in-flight neck cushion that was such a cumbersome contraption the user would end up looking like a prisoner being restrained for the duration of the flight! Hardly a glamorous travel accessory. Another idea so bad you can't believe anyone thought there was a business in it was the bed linen with a line down the middle to stop arguments about who was sleeping on whose side of the bed! That was one investment none of us were willing to get into bed with.

It took several seasons for me to come across a worse invention than the cardboard beach furniture we were asked to invest in during the first series. 'What happens if my little boy Tom comes out of the sea and sits on it?' I asked, perfectly reasonably. The inventor told me to control my son and not to let him! I thought she compounded a bad idea with a poor attitude.

Eventually though, a truly appalling idea came before us and it remains possibly the daftest idea we've ever had in the Den: a glove. Not a pair of gloves, a single glove. The 'inventor' thought that wearing a glove on the right hand would remind British drivers driving on the Continent to drive on the right and thus reduce accidents. Or was it the left side because there's no glove on that hand? I'm confused. Help. Oh, I've crashed.

Aside from the fact that, like the cucumber condom, there wasn't a great need for a device to remind travelling Brits which side of the road to drive on; and quite apart from the fact that the device he had come up with was potentially dangerous; the truly daft part of his idea was that we all own a pair of gloves already. If any individual thinks this might work for them, they can simply choose to wear half of a pair of gloves they already own. No one would pay for a specially made and specially packaged driving glove when they can buy a pair of gloves for a couple of quid in most street markets in the country. It was just preposterous!

But highly entertaining.

Ask around

Throughout these sorts of presentations I find myself wondering, 'Why didn't someone stop them? Surely there must be someone in their life with a tiny bit of common sense who could have taken them to one side and said, "Really, have you thought about this properly?"' Not only had these people had these bad ideas and mistaken them for businesses, they had wasted time and money on them. And presumably, a few months and several thousands pounds down, no one had the heart to tell them they were deluded . . . until they met the Dragons.

So how can you be sure that you aren't about to spend your time and your money on a bad idea? Well you could try asking people for their opinion. Some entrepreneurs are deluded into thinking their bad idea is potentially so lucrative that they won't tell people about it in case the idea gets stolen! The chances that someone will steal your idea are so remote that it really is a risk worth taking. Remember the old saying: no risk, no reward? Take a small risk and reap a big reward. And if you really can't face telling friends and family, find an online forum and ask for feedback.

The other technique is to force yourself to come up with five reasons why your idea will fail in the marketplace. Then take a long hard look at those five reasons and ask yourself how likely it is that these scenarios would happen. A bit likely? Pretty likely? Very likely? And those are just the reasons you came up with. There are hundreds more you haven't considered yet.

MISTAKE 5

Right idea, wrong person. Or, right person, wrong idea

THIS IS ANOTHER COMMON MISTAKE WE SEE IN THE DEN every series, if not every day of filming: a complete mismatch between the idea and the person trying to turn it into a business.

Welcome to the competition

A good example of this are the people who invent toys and games. Every couple of years there seems to be a craze around a new game – it's happened with Rubik's Cube, Trivial Pursuit, Buzz Lightyear toys and Bratz dolls, and it will keep on happening. The right toy can be incredibly lucrative. Trouble is, this is such a competitive market and there are so many toys and games out there that the chances that your game will be the big hit next Christmas – even if it really is as good as you say it is – are incredibly small. And there's a very good reason for that: nearly all the really big games and puzzles are made by a very small number of manufacturers.

Take a look at the board games in your house right now. I bet that most if not all of them are made by Waddingtons, Parker Brothers or Mattel. And Parkers and Mattel are subsidiaries of the same company! My point is that it is very difficult for new entrants into the toy market to have a really big hit. Deborah Meaden invested in something called the YouDoo Doll that you can make yourself. Even with her contacts and marketing expertise – not to mention the publicity from being on the Den – the YouDoo Doll remains a very small business. Therefore I would say that unless you work for one of those toy manufacturers, you are probably the wrong person to be taking your brilliant game to the market.

This advice holds true for so many other industries as well. Time and again we see Den hopefuls who think they can take on dominant market players, but history tells us that they almost certainly can't. Nevertheless, these entrepreneurs spend their time and money getting prototypes made, even ordering thousands of products on the off chance they'll get distribution, when – statistically – they don't stand a chance.

Matching skills and opportunity

As investors, we Dragons are all very good at spotting an opportunity that's right for us as individuals. It's not surprising that Peter Jones pays attention when a technological business comes before us – he is Mr Technology. Nor is it a surprise that Theo Paphitis sees retail opportunities that the rest of us don't:

he's Mr High Street. We instinctively know if a business is a good fit for us, and we can also instinctively tell if the person matches the opportunity they are presenting to us. Sometimes the mismatch is so great that the chance of turning their idea into a business is virtually zero. As an investor, I look for businesses where the skills of the people involved in the venture match the opportunity in front of them. Skills on their own don't make a business, and neither does opportunity. But where you get a fit between the skills and the opportunity, then you have a really good chance of building a successful business.

Let me give you some examples to show what I mean. Let's just say that a group of teenage girls think there's a need among other teenage girls for a magazine about computer games. Now, as the father of five girls, I might think that was an interesting proposition: after all, girls play games almost as much as boys, but virtually all the marketing, all the programming, all the websites and magazines are aimed at boys. Gaming for girls? That sounds like an opportunity.

So then I'd look at the girls who wanted to launch the magazine, and although they know an awful lot about gaming, and even though they know everything about being a teenage girl, they don't know anything about launching a magazine. They might be able to write an article, but could they commission photographers, sell advertising space or negotiate distribution? Do they know anything about libel laws? It's pretty clear that there is a disastrous mismatch between the (lack of) skills and the opportunity. And that means there's no business. That's an extreme illustration, but I hope it makes my point.

It can work in the reverse too. If you've seen a lot of the

Den, then you've probably seen several situations where one or other of the Dragons have said to an inventor: 'I'm not willing to invest in this product, but I am willing to invest in you.' That's because, generally speaking, good inventors tend to also be serial inventors, just as good entrepreneurs are serial entrepreneurs – of course that doesn't mean the next idea they have is the one that will make money. If we can do a deal that gives us a stake in a very able inventor's future ideas, then we'll be more likely to invest. For me the frustrating thing about Den presentations like these is that I can see there are some very able people wasting time, effort and money on the wrong idea when – if they had just analysed their idea a bit more rigorously – they could already have embarked on a much more prosperous venture.

So what should you do if you've got a brilliant idea and you're smart enough to realise that you're not the right person to make a success of it? Simple: you need to share your idea with someone who is the right person. I know a lot of people are unwilling to do this because they fear their idea will be stolen, but what they don't realise is that unless they share it, all they have is an idea. Ask yourself this: would you rather own 100 per cent of an idea or a percentage of a business? It's a pretty easy answer, isn't it? The follow-up question isn't quite so easy: would you rather own 50 per cent of that business or 1 per cent? The right answer is almost always 1 per cent. Let me explain . . .

> 66 Ideas are cheap. Effort is how you create wealth. 99

You've probably heard the phrase that success is 1 per cent inspiration and 99 per cent perspiration. It gets repeated so often because it is so often true. And that means that if all you are contributing to a venture is the idea, then it's fair to argue that your stake in it should be just 1 per cent. The idea is actually a very small part of any business, and therefore a small component of any business's success: it all comes down to brilliant execution. I'm sure lots of people have had the idea of opening a health club in their local area, but I'm the one who put the work in and actually opened a health club. Ideas are cheap, but effort is how you create wealth.

So imagine for a second that you have a brilliant idea for a board game. Realistically you've got three routes to getting your game to market.

Route 1

You go it alone. Get it made, get it distributed, and try and make a profit after your enormous set-up costs.

Route 2

Call up Waddingtons and tell them you've got a great idea for a game and you'll let them have a 50 per cent stake.

Route 3

Call up Waddingtons and tell them you've got a great idea for a game and all you want is to earn a 1 per cent royalty on any sales.

Which of those three options is most likely to result in the receptionist putting your call through to the right department and your game becoming a success? It's Route 3, isn't it? Route 1 is implausible and Route 2 is unattractive to your potential partner who's already got a big enough slice of the games market without you. I'll say it again: if you're not the right person, you don't have a business. Which is why 1 per cent of someone else's business is more lucrative than 100 per cent of your idea.

> **"** If you can't come up with an original idea, copy someone else's! **"**

If your problem is that you are a great entrepreneur who's lacking a great idea, I have some very valuable advice for you too: just copy someone else's business. None of my businesses – selling ice creams, operating care homes and nurseries, running health clubs – were original ideas, but they were all fantastic businesses.

Case study 1: Flooz

Back in the late 1990s, the internet was a bit like a virtual Wild West. There was a massive 'land grab' going on as hungry new hustlers vied for their place in the promised land of e-commerce. And just like the real Wild West, the speculators were miles ahead of the law enforcers. People weren't sure if statutory rights were enforceable online, or what kind of protection they'd have from fraudsters, and so the banks – who were slow to offer their own services online – recommended their customers used extreme caution when handing over their credit card details to a dotcom.

In fact, there was so much widespread fear about revealing your financial details that several companies came up with an innovative solution: an online currency. One of those companies was Flooz. com.

At Flooz.com you could exchange real currency for floozes which you would then use to buy products on other websites. This meant you only had to trust your financial information to Flooz.com. To make themselves seem respectable and worthy of your trust, they ran an expensive series of adverts starring Whoopi Goldberg. The advertising campaign was paid for with around $35 million of venture capital.

I cannot think of a more difficult business to get off the ground, for several reasons. First of all, you have to convince the public to buy floozes; secondly, you have to convince retailers to accept floozes; thirdly, you have to encourage people to buy online (which was still a novelty when it launched in 1998); and fourth, you have to sell the idea that what the world really needs is a new currency. Called flooz *of all things. To make it even harder, the flooz wasn't the only online currency launched in the dotcom frenzy – you could also have paid for your purchases with beenz. A rival really wasn't* something Flooz.com could cope with and in 2001, the business was wound up.

Flooz was actually a pretty well-run business. It had an able team who managed to convince some pretty impressive partners to accept floozes, including Tower Records and Barnes & Noble. The directors might have whizzed through their venture capital money, but they really had no option but to spend hard and fast on a big ad campaign as they needed that visibility to reassure users. So what was their big mistake?

The major problem with Flooz.com was revealed the very moment the business launched. Someone forgot to ask the most basic of questions: is this a good idea? Had someone taken a minute to do just that, then all that venture capital could have been put into something that might have stood a chance of producing a return.

I accept that it's hard to remember exactly what it was like in the 1990s and that there were genuine concerns about the safety of online shopping at the time that we've since forgotten about. I also accept that when someone first had the idea of an internet currency it seemed like the answer to a pretty big problem. But what I can't accept is that no one involved in the venture said: does the world really need this? Or that someone else didn't ask: won't the banks get their act together and put a lot of money and effort into online security sometime soon? Did no one ask if they really could take on some of the biggest and richest corporations in the world? And why didn't anyone involved in the organisation notice that Flooz is one of the worst brand names you've ever heard of?

It really didn't matter what happened after the business was launched, or how well it was managed. Nothing could compensate for the fact that it was just a very, very bad idea. Unsurprisingly, competitor Beenz.com went bust in the same month.

MISTAKE 6

Inadequate research

IN SERIES 8 OF *DRAGONS' DEN*, AN ENTREPRENEUR CALLED Tony Curtis came to see us. He had developed heated gloves for playing rugby. He had acquired patents, made proto- types and gone into production with a glove with specially adapted fingers that meant the wearer could still catch a rugby ball.

My problem with his business wasn't that rugby players represent a pretty small market, because I felt the gloves could be adapted for other sports. Nor was my problem that heated gloves were readily available in department stores. The fact that it wasn't the most defendable product in the world – there was nothing to prevent an existing player like Adidas or Reebok bringing out their own version – wasn't my prob- lem with the idea either. My problem was that I had just come back from a skiing holiday where I had been wearing heated skiing gloves that were effectively identical to Tony Curtis's glove.

When I told Tony this, it appeared he didn't want to believe me. He insisted that his glove was different to anything else on the market. The fact that I had used a virtually identical glove just a few days before was something he would not accept. Even if I had liked the product, I didn't like my honesty and integrity being called into question and so I declared myself out.

Don't stop researching your market

In the car back home after filming that day, I actually felt a bit sorry for Tony because I completely understood how he'd spent countless hours and a substantial amount of money on his gloves. When you start a business, it takes over your life. For months, if not years, all you can think about is spreadsheets, meetings, orders, payments and the hundred other things you have to juggle in the early days. Even though Tony had kept several juggling balls in the air, he had let one of them drop: research.

I believe him when he says he had researched the market before he embarked on his venture, but the problem he had was that he stopped doing his research. In the years between him thinking a heated rugby glove was a good idea and him having his product ready for the market, someone else had got their product into the shops. Tony's glove didn't stand a chance.

> 66 *Good research stops you wasting time, effort and money.* 99

Good research stops you from wasting time, effort and money on a doomed venture. Inadequate research is one of the biggest mistakes businesses make, and quite frankly it's inexcusable.

Tony is certainly not the only person to leave the Den without investment because of poor research. While he had failed to spot a rival, others had failed to spot a change in the law that would have made their product unviable (for instance, a device to clean oil-based paints when legislation will soon limit the use of oil-based paints), or a change in technology, or the market, or in demand or in their supply chain. To start a business with confidence, and to run a business with optimism, you need to know you've covered all your bases.

What you need to know

When launching a new business I would break down the areas you need to research as follows:

1. Revenue streams

By far the most important aspect of any business is the way it earns money. The first thing an entrepreneur needs to be sure of is that they've maximised their income. Give some thought as to all the ways your business can secure revenue from your customers. A hairdresser, for example, will make the most of their money cutting hair, but selling beauty products, offering head massages or doing hair and make-up for weddings might bring in additional revenues. At Bannatyne Health Clubs, by far the bulk of our income comes from membership subscriptions, but we have additional revenues from our cafés, spas and merchandising. A new business doesn't want to miss out on precious revenue, so make sure you research all your potential sources of income.

2. Costs

I reckon that at least half of all business plans I see overlook a major cost. Whether it's business rates, VAT or the founder's salary, missing expenditure can frequently be enough to send a business into the red. Some costs, like premises and staff, are pretty obvious, but others, like service charges and employers' national insurance contributions, are not. New entrepreneurs are often very good at identifying the obvious costs but frequently lack the experience to anticipate the hidden costs of running a business. You need to thoroughly research your costs to be sure that your business planning is sound. We'll discuss costs in more detail later.

3. Rivals

Identifying your rivals – and your potential rivals – is absolutely key to success. Let's say you want to open an off-licence in your town: who are your rivals going to be? Pretty obviously, any other off-licences in town, but off-licences in neighbouring towns could also take some of your market share if they have good products, service and prices. As could the pubs and corner shops. And then there are the online wine retailers, the bulk sellers like Majestic, the national chains like Oddbins and the wine clubs. And then, of course, your biggest rival will almost certainly be your local supermarket. Think you've identified all your rivals? Think again. As soon as you open your doors, you will alert others to the potential for a new off-licence in your town. Is there anyone who would try and open in opposition to you? A national chain keen not to let the business of a town like yours fall into the hands of an independent trader, for example?

Whatever business you're in, you'll have rivals. And to compete with your rivals you need information about their business. You get this information by reading trade magazines and websites, by reading the financial pages and by networking. You can also get rivals' accounts from Companies House or, if they're a plc, from the Stock Exchange.

4. Customers

Really successful businesses really know their customers. They know what their customers want, when they want it and how they want it. Anticipating what the market wants and delivering it at just the right moment is a fundamental of business success.

You can get to know your customers by reading about them, hanging out with them in local bars and cafés, surveying them and through statistical research. The Office of National Statistics (www.statistics.gov.uk) has all sorts of demographic data gleaned from the census and surveys that you can use to understand who your customers are, where they live and how much money they've got to spend. You can use this information to estimate the potential size of your customer base. If you know your customer, you know your market.

Your product

Whether you offer a physical product or a service, it's your job to know everything there is to know about it. I know what the trends in fitness are, what the new machines for next year will be and who will be making them. I'm in the fitness industry, so I *know* the fitness industry. One of my *Dragons' Den* investments was in an entrepreneur called Peter Moule who is a specialist in electronics. Peter *knows* electronics. He knows how his products are made, how they are used and why they are important. His product knowledge was one of the many reasons why he got my investment.

These are the big areas you need to research, but you also need to be sure of your facts on relevant legislation, tax implications and the state of the economy. And of course, as Tony Curtis learned too late with his rugby glove, you need to keep doing your research. Markets don't stay still, so neither should your research.

MISTAKE

Thinking your customers are just like you

MOST PEOPLE I KNOW HAVE A DREAM BUSINESS THAT they'd like to start. My wife's dream was always to open a 'restaurant with rooms'. It would be a great venue, with a terrific wine list, the best food for miles around and, if you'd had a bit too much to drink, you could take a room upstairs and stay over and sample a traditional cooked breakfast in the morning. It sounded great. It sounded exactly like the sort of place that we would like to hang out with our friends.

For years Joanne and I looked for the right premises, and we eventually found a rundown hotel in our home town of Darlington. It seemed perfect. We spent a fortune on the renovation (still a sore point in the Bannatyne household!), hired a first-class chef and opened for business.

The first few nights went well. Our friends came, we got rip-roaring drunk on superb wines, ate some fantastic food and even got some good reviews in the local press. But there were only so many times that our friends were going to eat in our restaurant each month, and it quickly became clear that there weren't enough people in Darlington who wanted experimental haute cuisine. To put it simply: there weren't enough people like us to make Joanne's dream into a business.

After losing money for several months, we made changes. The new menu consisted of more traditional dishes, the portion size increased to offer better value for money and the wines dropped a price bracket. We also changed the entire focus of the business: instead of running a restaurant with rooms, the business became a hotel with a restaurant. It was such a successful switch that we built an extension to add more rooms, and that worked out so well that I now own several hotels around the country.

Others who realise too late that there aren't enough customers like them don't get the chance to turn things round.

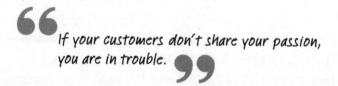

If your customers don't share your passion, you are in trouble.

Businesses with physical premises that rely on a local clientele to survive are particularly vulnerable to this trap. Restaurant and bar premises frequently change hands because one restaurateur after another opens a place that's right for them, but not for their customers. Retail businesses often make this mistake too: clothing shops, record shops, cupcake shops and the like are often so clearly stamped with the owner's taste and preferences that they are either too niche for the general public, or too off-putting. It doesn't matter how passionate you are about your business: if your customers don't share your passion, then you're in trouble. There are, however, several ways you can make sure this doesn't happen to your business.

1   The first and most important way is to *have sales targets*. If you have planned your business properly, you'll know how many sales you need to make each week or each month to turn a profit. If you miss that target in your first month, that might be understandable, but if you keep missing it then you need to take action. Targets and benchmarks are the tools that will stop you going too far into the red.

2   *Speak to your customers.* Find any way you can to get close to the people who will use your business. Ask them to fill in surveys. Have a suggestions box. Encourage them to send you emails. Use Twitter and Facebook to have a dialogue with them. Find out what they really want and how much they want to pay for it.

3   *Get your stock control right.* If you're in retail, holding too much stock can be expensive; holding too much of the wrong stock can be fatal. If you can't take stock on a 'sale or return' basis, you need to have a strategy for selling it on if your customers don't want to buy it from you so that you can get some of your money

back. And you need to be brutal: if something doesn't sell at the beginning, you can be pretty sure it's never going to sell. Fashion retailers are particularly vulnerable to this.

Of course, there is one place where niche businesses flourish, and that's the internet. Specialist retailers are no longer reliant on a local customer base for their sales. Jazz record shops, fly fishing outlets and hobby shops can get orders from all over the world.

New mums Justine Roberts and Carrie Longton instinctively knew there were other women like them out there, women who were stuck at home with valid opinions and niggling concerns about how to raise their children. If they had opened a coffee shop and waited for these women to appear, they'd have been lucky to have had a couple of hundred customers a week. Instead, they opened a virtual coffee shop online: mumsnet.com. It now has 1.25 million unique users every month and has become one of the most powerful websites in Britain. If you need to find customers who are just like you, you could do worse than following Justine and Carrie's example and look to start your business online.

MISTAKE 8

If I build it, they will come

IN 1989 A FILM CAME OUT STARRING KEVIN COSTNER called *Field of Dreams*. Despite being utterly preposterous to my mind, it was one of the biggest movies of the year. The storyline was this: Kevin Costner's character, a corn farmer, kept hearing a voice in his head that said: 'If you build it, he will come.' For some reason he felt sure that the voice was telling him to dig up his corn field (instantly reducing next year's harvest, and therefore profits!) and build a baseball diamond. If he did this, he felt sure famous – but dead – baseball players would come and play a game in his field. Of course, this being a Hollywood movie, that's exactly what did happen and Kevin's character got to play with the ghosts of his long-dead heroes.

As I say, the premise is ridiculous, but clearly not everyone feels the same way, because the 'if I build it, he will come' belief seems pretty widespread among inexperienced entrepreneurs.

Let's start by looking at the retail sector. About six months ago, a nail bar opened in a town near where I live. As someone who owns several spas, both in my health clubs and my hotels, I pay attention when I see a new entrant into the health and beauty sector.

The nail bar owner had completely refitted the premises – it had previously been a stationery shop – and invested in specialist equipment. I thought their décor looked a bit garish and amateurish, but I reasoned that I wasn't the target market for a nail bar and was willing to accept that the bright pink would attract the customers they were after.

Every week or so, I would drive past it and always slowed down to see how many customers were getting a manicure. I hardly ever saw anyone in there. I asked my wife, my daughters and staff if they had been in there: they hadn't even heard of it. These women were that nail bar's target market and they didn't know it existed. The sloppy paint job was not the reason the place was failing.

I became quite fixated on the state of this nail bar – when you love business as much as I do, this is the kind of thing you do for fun – and started calculating how much money the nail bar was losing. I had a good idea how much rent it would pay, how steep its rates were and, as there were always two members of staff in there, I reckoned it was costing between four and five grand a month to stay open. Unsurprisingly, after six months – probably when there was a break clause in its lease – it went out of business.

The people who opened that nail bar made the classic 'if I build it' mistake. They could have leafleted every house in the area for a few hundred quid. They could have put posters in their window advertising opening offers, they could have advertised in the local paper or stood on the street handing out flyers. They did none of these things and the customers never came.

It's a trap lots of retailers fall into. They think that because hundreds of people walk past their door every day that those same hundreds of people will pop in. The reality is that a) most of those people won't even notice you've opened, b) many of them won't care, c) some of them will wait to hear recommendations about you from their friends or in newspapers before popping in, and d) the rest are waiting for an invitation to come in. Handing out flyers with a time-limited discount on them is the commercial version of sending out invitations to a party.

Take a proactive approach

If retail outlets in prime locations can suffer if they don't do any marketing, imagine how tough it is for retailers in side streets or away from main shopping areas. If you open a shop in a sub-prime area because you don't want to pay high rents, then your marketing doesn't just have to tell people that you've opened for business, it has to be so compelling that it convinces customers to go out of their way to try you. You can even say on your flyers: 'We don't pay high rents, so you won't pay high prices' and make a virtue out of your location.

When we open a new health club, we advertise locally, we have introductory offers, open days and we can also reduce or waive the joining fee to encourage people to sign up. Within a few weeks of opening, there won't be many people in town who don't know about us.

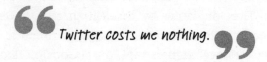

" Twitter costs me nothing. "

Marketing doesn't have to be expensive. You don't need to take out radio ads or pay for billboards. I've never done a national advertising campaign for my health clubs because local ads are more effective and less expensive. One of the most successful ways I promote my clubs and hotels these days is via Twitter. I recently tweeted a 2-for-1 offer at our spas and we sold dozens in a single day. Twitter costs me nothing.

If the owners of that nail bar had gone on Facebook and searched for local women, local mums' groups or businesses with a large female workforce, they could have reached thousands of potential customers within a few hours. The mantra shouldn't be, 'If I build it, they will come,' it should be, 'When I build it, I will bloody well make sure I will tell the world about it.'

Being found online

The Kevin Costner trap is particularly easy to fall into if your business is online. When you don't have the overheads of premises or a large staff, it's very easy to sit at your desk and design and tweak your website until it is absolutely perfect because you aren't burning too much cash. Every day, in fact probably every minute, someone launches an absolutely perfect website . . . that no one visits.

Getting online customers can be extremely hard. I have no idea how many websites there are out there – tens of millions no doubt – and getting people to visit you rather than your rivals is made a lot harder by the fact that most web users choose one particular search engine to guide them round the web. If you can't get a high rank on a Google search, your business could be in trouble.

There are entire books, and indeed entire industries, devoted to 'Search Engine Optimisation' because businesses are learning that getting a high Google ranking is worth paying for. Understanding how Google searches for and ranks websites is crucial if you're going to make it on to the first page of results. Understanding how your customers will search for you will also make a difference. They're unlikely to search for 'Jenny's Shoe Shop' but they might search for 'cheap shoes in the UK', and that means you need to tailor your content to attract Google users.

Marketing matters

I think most new entrepreneurs underestimate how important marketing is for their business. The more time I've spent in business, the more I realise how vital it is. Whether you are networking at industry events, taking part in PR stunts or paying for adverts, telling people about your business is just as important as making your product, selling your service or doing your accounts. I'd go further: unless people know about your business, you don't need to bother doing any of those other things. Let me tell you: if all you do is build it, no one will come.

MISTAKE

Avoiding the difficult tasks

IMAGINE YOU'RE SETTING UP A POTTERY BUSINESS. YOU'RE an expert in ceramics and you want to start selling your own designs but you have no experience of working for yourself. What's the first thing you're going to do: find premises? Negotiate supply deals with local retailers? Arrange a demonstration at a local event? Register for VAT? Or make some pottery?

And once you've made some pottery, it's possible you might just make some more – after all, people need to see a wide range of work, in a wide range of colours – before you take on any of the other tasks that are all an essential part of running a successful business.

People who have worked in a sector for several years, whether they're software designers, electrical engineers or vets, often think they can do a better job than their employer.

They probably can – after all, they understand their industry inside out – but it's also very easy for 'experts' to concentrate on the thing they do well to the exclusion of the other tasks needed to run a profitable business.

In the Den, although people say they're looking for investment, what many are actually looking for is help. They want a Dragon to step in and take on the tasks they don't feel able to do themselves. Although I don't sympathise, I do understand. If you're a leader in your field, you've probably got quite used to feeling in control, having your opinion valued or getting away with less effort than was required earlier in your career. The psychology is pretty simple: when such experts take on the new and unfamiliar tasks of running a business – like paperwork or sales or finances – they feel awkward and unsure. Conversely, when they concentrate on their area of expertise, they feel powerful, capable and comfortable. So they respond by focusing on their specialist area even more, and continue to neglect the rest of their business. I have noticed that these kinds of entrepreneurs are also often too proud to ask for help . . . and so they ask the Dragons for money instead.

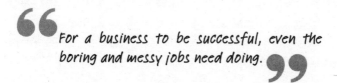

> For a business to be successful, even the boring and messy jobs need doing.

Everyone enjoys aspects of their business more than others, and everyone is better at some tasks than others, but for a business to be successful, even the boring jobs and the messy ones and especially the difficult ones need doing as well as the fun ones. At home, you can get away with not fixing the guttering or not replacing loose carpet or ignoring your paperwork, but in business those things don't just lose you customers, they are also in breach of legislation!

How to get everything done

The best way of making sure the jobs you don't want to do get done is to be part of a team. As businesses grow, it's accepted that some people will specialise in sales or accounts or manufacturing. While some businesses are successfully launched as one-person outfits, if you know that you don't have all the necessary skills to make a success of yours, then you probably need to find yourself a partner or an employee whose skills complement your own.

If that's not an option, then you need to devise a strategy for making sure that those less attractive tasks still get done. Here are my suggestions; hopefully one of them will work for you.

1   It's a ridiculously simple idea, but *make a list of all the jobs you need to do.* Sometimes seeing things in black and white can make them more real, and more manageable. Write a number next to each task in order of its priority, then simply work through the tasks.

2   *Allocate time to do the task.* I recommend new entrepreneurs set aside a specific time to do their accounts each week as it's the best way to check on the progress of a new business (and because it's something most people find difficult at first). However, others hide

behind their spreadsheets and don't get on to the tasks they fear. Whatever is your bogey task, put some time in your diary to tackle it.

3 *Impose a deadline for getting it done.* Some people don't do their tax return until HM Revenue & Customs start charging penalties. Deadlines are a very effective tool for getting things done. The best way to impose a deadline on your task is to tell someone else that it'll be done by a certain date. If you know a client, a colleague or your bank manager is waiting for you to do something, you'll be far more motivated to get it done.

4 *Impose a penalty.* Tell yourself you can't do any more of the fun stuff until you've tackled the difficult stuff. Make a pact with yourself that you won't go to the pub, watch the football or get a take-away until the task is done.

5 *Invent a reward.* Promise yourself that if you do attend to the difficult stuff, you will go to the pub, watch the match, get a take-away etc. Penalties work for some people, others are motivated by rewards.

MISTAKE 10

Hiding behind your desk

REMEMBER HIDING BEHIND THE SOFA AS A KID WHEN *Dr Who* was on? Believe it or not, some adults find business so scary they continue to hide behind the furniture.

We have become so used – so quickly – to communicating via emails and texts that a lot of people have become uncomfortable with face-to-face communication. I've read about parents that only speak to their teenagers via Facebook, so it's no wonder that some people would rather do their business communication via LinkedIn than by picking up the phone.

Technology has transformed the way we do business. Often, the first place customers are directed to find out more information about a company is a website; we have teleconferences with overseas colleagues and clients; and office gossip is now silently communicated via email. Technology makes it very easy to forget that the fundamental rules of business haven't changed: business is still about two people, or two parties, exchanging payment for goods and services rendered. In other words: business is still about relationships.

The importance of relationships

This is especially true for new businesses. When no one has ever heard of you and you have no track record, the strength of your relationships with clients and suppliers will be the foundation of your fledgling business. Let me demonstrate: imagine for a second that you run a business that is facing financial difficulties and you can't pay all your bills. You have to choose between paying the invoice of the person you've looked in the eye, shaken hands with and maybe had lunch with, or paying the invoice of the person you've never met. I know which invoice I'd be more likely to pay.

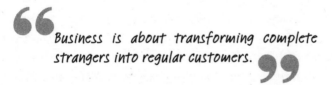

Business is about transforming complete strangers into regular customers.

At its most fundamental level, the art of business is simply about transforming complete strangers into regular customers. The job of the entrepreneur, then, is to meet as many strangers as possible. We've all received emails and cold calls from people we don't know. We know from experience how easy it is either to ignore or forget about those emails and not to return those phone messages. Yet many new entrepreneurs think sending out blanket emails will bring them customers. I've even been told by one entrepreneur that they knew people were too busy to take their calls during the day, so they deliberately called in the evening when they knew they would be able to leave a message! If you want to be ignored, it's a terrific strategy.

Whatever your business, you need to find a way of meeting the people who will be your clients, suppliers and customers. When I built my first care home, the most important people I needed to have a relationship with were the team in the local planning department. The plans needed council approval and every stage of the construction had to be inspected by the building control officers. Like most people, I had never dealt with these departments before, but as soon as I realised the power they had over my ambitions, I made sure I got to know them. I invited officers from the planning department on site visits and asked for their advice. I also attended the meetings of the planning committee at the council offices. As the construction went on, it became easy to phone them up to ask questions or resolve disputes. By the time I was building my fourth and fifth care homes, I knew them pretty well and – more importantly – they knew me. They knew I worked with reputable builders, they knew I played by the rules and their site visits got shorter and shorter, therefore taking up less of my time. This wasn't about buttering them up, or getting in a position to curry favour, it was simply about my finding out what they needed and what their priorities were, and them getting to know my requirements and priorities.

In the early days of a business when you don't have an established track record, potential customers and clients need to see you've got integrity instead. The way people do that is by looking you in the eye and shaking you by the hand. For that to happen, you obviously have to stop hiding behind your desk.

I have a few suggestions of ways you can meet people in your industry, and a few more for ways to meet potential customers. First, how to make industry contacts:

1. Chamber of Commerce

Your local chamber of commerce will meet regularly to discuss issues of importance to local businesses. At chamber meetings you will get to talk to other entrepreneurs, probably a few bank managers and local officials and find out if you can help each other out. Even if these people aren't in your field – and in some ways, you'll be hoping they're not – they can still become powerful advocates for you and your business once they get to know you.

2. Trade events

Although these can be expensive to attend, they are a great way of meeting people face to face. Everyone wears name badges and the whole point of attending them is to network, so there's no reason not to walk up to a stranger and introduce yourself. Some of the best networking, unsurprisingly, happens at the bar! And even if you don't get to meet the person you were hoping to talk to, you get to send them an email afterwards saying, 'I'm really sorry I didn't get to meet you at the event, I really wanted to talk to you about X and was hoping you might take a look at this . . .'

3. Trade newspapers, magazines and websites

OK, not technically a way of meeting people, but following news and events in your industry is the best way of making sure you have something relevant to say when you do meet people. You will also find out about upcoming events through these sources, and often the earlier you book for something, the cheaper it is to attend.

Depending on your business, your customers may have nothing to do with your industry. I wouldn't expect to find too many of my members attending fitness industry events, for example. So meeting potential customers might require a separate strategy.

Meeting your customers

Think about the places where your potential customers are likely to be, and wherever they are, you need to be there too. Are there local events where you can have a stall; or can you have an open day and invite people to come and have a look around? Can you stand in the street wearing a sandwich board and handing out leaflets? The great thing about meeting customers face to face isn't just that they get to know you, it's that you get to understand what they need and can tailor your business to appeal to them.

Of course, it is possible to do business entirely online these days and never meet your suppliers or your customers. There will still be online forums where you can share information, observe your customers and ask them for feedback. However, when things go wrong – as they inevitably do – they are always more quickly resolved via direct, personal contact. All businesses have glitches and rough patches, and when your customers encounter one of yours, you want to be able to deal with it quickly, which means that online businesses still need to answer the phone. Those businesses that hide behind automated customer service, phone trees and online FAQs are squandering the chance to have a relationship with their customers. Instead, customers experience a series of impersonal transactions, making it much easier for them to take their business elsewhere if they are not happy with your service. If customers have a relationship with you, they might just give you a second chance.

MISTAKE 11

Being stupid with equity

EVERY NOW AND THEN SOMEONE COMES INTO THE DEN and gets an offer of investment but still walks away without it. Why? Often because they are greedy with equity.

I understand why entrepreneurs are reluctant to give away large stakes in their companies, but there have been a few times when I've sat on the sidelines watching another Dragon negotiate with an entrepreneur and wanted to get up and the shake the stupidity out of the entrepreneur. 'Don't you realise,' I want to say to them, 'that if you give a Dragon 40 or 50 per cent of your company, the chance that your business will succeed increases by hundreds of per cent. Thousands maybe. Not only that, but you'll learn loads.'

The chance to run your company alongside a Dragon for a few years is a priceless education in business, so naturally I think entrepreneurs who walk away from that chance are bonkers. If they worked with a Dragon for a few years, they could gain invaluable knowledge and experience and then use that to start a really big business that they could keep 100 per cent of. However, being greedy with equity isn't the only way to be stupid with it. I'd now like to talk you through the ways that not understanding the value of equity can damage your business.

Greed

As I say, I understand why entrepreneurs don't want to give away equity in their company – after all, it's something they've nurtured and spent months if not years working on. They may also have put a considerable amount of their own money into it. It's natural for them to feel a profound sense of ownership.

The language we use – *giving away* equity – doesn't help because in fact, the equity is *exchanged* for investment. And that investment will represent money and expertise from someone who will become a partner in your business. If you're smart, you'll want your partner to care almost as much about your business as you do. If they only have a 5 per cent stake, they won't stand to make a great return, and so they won't be motivated to nurture and grow your business. However, if an investor has a meaningful stake in the venture, you'll have their attention and passion as well as their money.

It might help to think about the value of your stake in the company, rather than the size of it. Let's say you have a business worth £100,000 (I'll come on to how you should accurately value your company in a later chapter), and you seek outside investment of £100,000. Once you have the investor's cash in your business, it will be worth £200,000, so if your stake in the company drops to 50 per cent it doesn't matter because the *value* of your stake is still the £100,000 you started negotiations with.

Generosity

This might sound odd coming from an investor, but you can also make a mistake by giving too much equity away. Large corporations often raise investment funds in stages: at the early stage, when the risk of failure is highest, an investor will ask for an equity percentage that reflects the risk; at the next stage, when the risks are lower but vast amounts of cash are needed to expand, entrepreneurs find they are asked to give away another large slice of their business in exchange for multimillion-pound investment. The difficulty isn't that the entrepreneur is left with a tiny stake, it's that if too much equity has been given away in the first round of fundraising, the business is less attractive to the institutional investors with the millions. This problem is exacerbated if the early investors have negotiated what is known as a 'non-dilution clause' which fixes the size of their stake, preventing it from being reduced in a second round of fundraising. If you think your business might need additional rounds of fundraising, then you need to be mindful of how future investors will view the stakes you give to early investors.

Stupidity

The size of someone's stake in your business should be an accurate reflection of that person's input, either in hours, money or some other contribution. If you share equity with other founders in your business, then it's important that you have an agreement setting out who does what – and how much of it – for their slice of the company. Letting dormant and lazy partners have too much of your company can cause the kind of resentment that leads to feuding and failing.

I've also heard of entrepreneurs who offer equity in their companies in lieu of payment. Obviously, as a last resort, this is better than going under, but as a long-term strategy it's nuts: 2 per cent here, 3 per cent there, 10 per cent to Uncle Fred, 5 per cent to Auntie May . . . you can end up frittering away your equity, and get lumbered with shareholders who offer the venture very little.

I was once asked to invest in a company whose founder thought he was being smart: instead of giving away equity in his business to family and friends who had invested nominal amounts, he had given away percentages in the company's income. By the time he came to me for several hundred thousand pounds of investment, he was only able to offer me a share of the 8 per cent of revenues he was still entitled to! Needless to say, I did not invest.

It is possible, with help from experienced incorporation specialists, to structure your company so that different sorts of investors have different sorts of shares. For example, some sorts of shares could entitle the holder to dividends, while some will be equity-only shares. Many companies have 'ordinary shares' and 'extraordinary shares' that have special clauses or restrictions attached to them.

When you give away equity in your company don't just think of the money you receive for that equity, think of the value the shareholder will add. And if they pressure you to give them more equity, then you need to explain that – as a prudent business owner – you are only considering the long-term position of the company, and therefore doing your best to protect their investments when you tell them they can't have any more!

Case study 2: Fashion Café

First there was the Hard Rock Café, an international chain where diners could ogle music memorabilia while they ate. Then came Planet Hollywood where the burgers were served against a backdrop of movie props and costumes. So why not the Fashion Café? Why couldn't that work too? How long have you got?

The café was the brainchild of Italian Tommaso Buti, one of those members of the fashion jet set whose actual day-job seems unclear but who always drives gorgeous cars and throws wonderful parties. He is one of those people whose primary skill is in bringing people together, a social networker of the highest calibre. His ability to sit still behind a desk and study a balance sheet is less well-known. On the one hand, Buti was the perfect guy to get a venture like the Fashion Café off the ground, on the other hand, well, he wasn't.

Most people think that the supermodels Claudia Schiffer, Naomi Campbell and Elle Macpherson were backers of the Fashion Café. The truth is the exact opposite; they were just the front. Instead of putting money into the venture, Buti paid them appearance fees for doing the publicity for his chain of cafés, for attending launches and occasionally dropping in like they owned the place. Their fees were reported to be $100,000 a pop, so when all three turned up at an event, it cost a lot of money. And they turned up a lot. He also agreed to pay them a tiny percentage of the takings.

The benefit of getting the supermodels to front the business was that it made it much easier to get backers. It's thought Buti raised about $30 million in venture capital from his friends in the fashion business and he set about opening cafés in New York, New Orleans and London. Now, I am not a great follower of fashion, but even I know New Orleans isn't famous for its couture. This was the first clue that there was a mismatch between the idea and the execution: something that was supposedly upmarket and exclusive was actually little more than a burger joint for day trippers to the French Quarter. In London, Buti bought a former nightclub in Leicester Square – again, not the most sophisticated neighbourhood – and spent millions renovating the place.

The London Fashion Café opened in November 1997, but by October 1998 it had already been placed into the hands of an administrator whose analysis of the business's failure was that it had cashflow problems. It had spent so much money on the renovations, that it could not meet its day-to-day costs.

So what was the biggest mistake the Fashion Café made? Was it Buti's apparent lack of financial management skills? Was it his lack of understanding of the importance of cashflow? Or was it the inescapable fact that a Fashion Café was just a bad idea?

In my opinion, I'm not sure even Donald Trump could have made a success of the Fashion Café. Sure, Buti's lack of spreadsheet skills didn't help, but the fundamental issue here is that it was a very bad idea. For starters, what is 'fashion memorabilia' and why would you want to pay to look at it? Secondly, there is a massive gulf between the image of haute couture and the touristy, theme-park restaurants they actually opened. And thirdly, when did you last see a supermodel eat a burger? They are infamous for not eating, let alone for not eating burgers! Really, this was an idea that was never, ever going to work.

MISTAKE 12

Not putting your own money in

MOST OF THE MILLIONAIRES I KNOW GREW UP WITH VERY little. Like me, they left school with no qualifications and held no great hopes of climbing the corporate ladder.

When people don't fit into 'the system' it's not surprising that they look outside it for an income, which often means starting a business. When someone with no other career options starts a business, I find that they work much harder and with more determination than those entrepreneurs who know they can go back to 'the day job' and a regular salary. If you've got no choice but to make a success of your business, the chances of your business becoming successful instantly multiply.

> *By putting your wealth, comfort and security on the line, you give yourself immense motivation to ensure your business doesn't fail.*

A very effective way of making sure that you have no choice but to make your business a success is by putting your own money into it. By putting your wealth, comfort and security on the line, you give yourself the most immense motivation to ensure that your business doesn't fail.

If you're lucky or smart enough to have significant savings, then putting in tens of thousands of pounds of your own money is bound to boost your determination levels, but I actually think it's much more effective to put in money you simply can't afford to lose. If you take out a loan, or increase your mortgage to put money into your business, you have a monthly bill that acts as a reminder of the commitment you have made and the risk you have taken. If the collapse of the business would see you in debt, believe me, you're not going to give up while there's even the remotest chance of getting your business into profit. An entrepreneur in debt is very often an entrepreneur in business.

In the Den, we frequently ask entrepreneurs how much of their own money they've put into a venture. You might have noticed that we are more inclined to put our own money into a business if the person leading it has already put a significant chunk of their own wealth into it. The reason for this is that entrepreneurs who aren't invested can walk away with far fewer consequences. If the economy hits a rough patch, or the market for their industry shifts, or they simply get exhausted or demoralised, there is not enough to stop them walking away.

While I would never want to encourage anyone to take on unnecessary debt, I would urge everyone in business to look at their personal level of investment, because it's usually when you have something to lose that you also stand to gain the most.

MISTAKE 13

Burning capital

YOU HAVE THE CHOICE BETWEEN TWO BUILDING FIRMS TO carry out renovations on your home: one comes with references, a fancy website and sends round uniformed workers to give you a quote; the other doesn't produce any results on a Google search. Which company are you going to use?

There are many ways we judge the companies we are thinking of doing business with. We might consider their brand, their offices or their website to try and see what sort of company they are and what sort of corporate values they have. And once we start to deal with a company, we continue to assess them by the level of service we get when we call reception, or the speed with which our invoices are paid. What we are doing when we assess companies like this is the business equivalent of being on a date and making judgements about a prospective partner on the basis of their clothes, their table manners and their conversational skills: we are assessing whether or not we want to have a relationship with that company.

All of which makes it very easy to understand why new companies are tempted to spend a lot of money on *looking like* an established company. Knowing full well that prospective customers will be judging them on their websites, offices and appearance, they shell out huge amounts of money on creating the appearance of a much bigger, more established and more successful company. Business cards, headed stationery, plush offices at a swish address, a professionally designed website, uniforms for employees, a fleet of expensive cars, amazing corporate gifts... there are plenty of things you can spend your money on, but they are no substitute for spending your time on developing a relationship with customers who can help you grow your business.

People are often quite surprised when they visit my office. For starters, it's in Darlington; secondly it's a very modest building; and thirdly, even though my office might be quite big, it's not decked out with executive toys and vast amounts of technology. What really surprises people is when I tell them it's a lot grander than my last HQ. And that office was a considerable step up from when I started Bannatyne Fitness: to begin with I worked on our dining table.

My current offices may not be impressive but they suit me and my company perfectly. I bought the property a few years ago because it's not very far from where I live, it's right next to one of my health clubs, and there was plenty of room for expansion. And of course, being in Darlington means I am not paying London salaries. Now that I spend a lot of time in London, either for filming or for business, I still have no need for a London office. Instead I have a flat in central London that I use for meetings, which saves on hotel costs for me and my team when we're in the capital.

What is impressive about my office is how cheap it was to buy, and how affordable it is to maintain. If you looked at my accounts, you would see just how smart a move my relatively low-key HQ really is. If my business – which has a turnover of around £100m a year – doesn't need a flash office, then I'm going to stick my neck out and say that no business needs to waste money on luxury premises.

Of course, it's not just offices and stationery that companies waste money on, it's employees too. Salaries make up the bulk of expenditure for most companies, and when you are paying salaries unnecessarily, it can really cost you. Taking on too many staff too soon can send you into the red and keep you there.

Let's just do a quick calculation for a start-up business. Let's say the company operates out of a small office that costs £1,500 a month and has three members of staff on £15k salaries. Once you've factored in the extra National Insurance contribution employers make, this new company's outgoings are around £5,500 a month, and that's before we've even mentioned utilities, insurance, stock, maintenance, computers and all the other things you start spending money on when you have premises and staff. This business would need to generate revenues of £7k or £8k a month to break even. Now let's say it takes six months for the business to start generating income. That's £33k the founders need to have on top of any start-up costs – like buying stock or getting a website built – before they stand a chance of getting a return on their investment. Entrepreneurs and investors often have conversations about 'burn rate', i.e., the speed with which companies spend their cash. The faster your burn rate, the quicker you can run into trouble.

How not to spend your capital

If you think spending £33k before you earn any revenue represents an alarming burn rate, then let me tell you about Boo.com, an online clothing retailer that raised £125 million in venture capital during the dotcom boom of the late 1990s, and spent it all in a little over six months. The founders spent millions getting the most spectacular website built. It was technically brilliant, but fundamentally flawed: at the time most internet users had super-slow dial-up connections and the Boo.com site took too long to load. They clicked away before they shopped.

The founders also spent – quite literally – a fortune on hotels and first-class travel, corporate gifts and funky offices. But the bulk of the cash went on two things: advertising and staff. They employed ad agencies to devise campaigns before the site was ready to launch and after launch they paid for primetime TV advertising. And as for the staff, it was estimated a business of Boo.com's size needed about 30 people – it employed 400.

When the business went into administration, it emerged that for all that outlay, Boo.com had managed to register just 300,000 users from whom they had generated £200,000 in turnover. That means that each user cost the company £416 to recruit and that they had spent an average of 66p. I wonder if the founders ever consider how differently they could have treated those 300,000 users: they could have built a site customers could actually use, offered prices they couldn't ignore and customer service they would have told their friends about. If they had done that, by now they might have been one of the world's biggest retailers. But they blew their cash and blew their chances.

> 66 If you can't control your costs, you won't control your profit. 99

Of course, this is an extreme example, but burning capital is still one of the most common reasons why otherwise decent and respectable companies go under. If you can't get your costs under control, you'll never be in control of your profits. The more you spend money on things you don't need, the less you will have of it for the things you do need, like unexpected bills, late payments on invoices, maternity leave or putting in an increased order in the run-up to Christmas.

Showing restraint

When I consider investing in a company, I look at the restraint the founders have shown with their expenditure. In the Den, we always ask people what they will do with the investment money if they are successful, and if they tell us that they're going to spend *our* money on *their* salary, it's never long before we declare ourselves out.

It just isn't necessary to spend money hand over fist to get a business off the ground. There are numerous inexpensive ways a new business can persuade customers to try the service out. Tempting prospective customers with discounts or staggered payments costs far less than an advertising campaign. Incentivising customers to recommend your services with a loyalty discount can spread the word about your service far more effectively than a publicity stunt.

> **66** *Every pound you spend unnecessarily is another pound you have to get your customers to give you.* **99**

Nor do you have to spend on offices and cars. Offer to travel to meet clients rather than have them come to you. Or hold your meetings in a coffee shop. When the founder of Cobra beer first started selling to Indian restaurants, he delivered the bottles himself out of the back of a VW Beetle that was falling apart: had he spent money on a posh delivery van and hired a driver, he might never have made sufficient profits to grow his business. These days, Karan Bilimoria is a multimillionaire with a seat in the House of Lords. He knew what all good entrepreneurs know: when you spend money on things that don't produce revenue, you make it very hard to turn a profit. Every pound you spend unnecessarily is another pound you have to get your customers to give you.

It might also help to learn and repeat the phrase 'fake it until you make it'. You don't have to have a call centre to sound professional on the phone; you don't have to have a Mayfair address when you can meet clients for a £5 coffee at the Ritz; you don't have to have a stockroom full of stock to take an order. I know of several entrepreneurs who were brilliant fakers when they started their businesses. One of them used to answer the phone in one accent, then put the caller through to 'the sales guy' who would have another accent, and have 'the accounts guy' chase the invoice. His clients never suspected he was just a one-man band!

MISTAKE

14

Deals, not relationships

PEOPLE ARE OFTEN SURPRISED WHEN I TELL THEM YOU don't have to be ruthless to be successful in business. Throughout my career, I've bought goods and services at prices people were prepared to sell them at, given contracts to people on the basis of the quotes they've given me and sold services at the prices that I've advertised. It's hardly ruthless and essentially boils down to a series of transparent and honest transactions.

Yet the idea that business is a cut-throat game persists. I love watching my friend Lord Sugar on *The Apprentice*, but I get a bit cross when the candidates that negotiate hardest with suppliers or sell the hardest to customers get all the praise. It might make good telly, but in my opinion as a long-term business strategy it's rubbish. Good business isn't just about brilliant deals, it's about mutually beneficial relationships.

Business only works if everyone makes their cut. And as most businesses buy and sell the same things month in, month out it makes a lot of sense to buy from the same people, and sell to the same people. If I negotiated too hard with my contractors every time we built a new health club, they would never tender for new contracts from me again. And that would mean that I was always having to interview and get to know new contractors. That takes up my time and costs me money. Far better to pay a decent price for a decent service and know that I have people who are always happy to work with me.

> 66
> *It costs far less to hold on to a customer than it does to find a new one.* 99

Similarly, if I tried to charge too much for memberships to my health clubs, members might start to question how much value they feel they get for their monthly subscription. I need my members to feel they're getting good value for money otherwise they will cancel their membership. Businesses often talk about the cost of 'client acquisition' – how much they have to spend on finding clients before the clients start spending with them – but they rarely talk about the cost of 'customer attrition'. It costs far less to hold on to a customer than it does to go out and find a new one, and that's why I believe that good relationships, not good deals, are at the heart of long-term business success.

Don't get me wrong, the ability to cut a good deal is an

essential tool of business, but be aware that sometimes you can cut too hard. In those circumstances, it's not just your adversary who gets injured.

MISTAKE 15

Not being hungry enough

THERE COMES A POINT IN THE LIFE OF JUST ABOUT EVERY
business where a sane person would walk away. Too much
debt, too many hours, too much hassle, just too damned hard.
And it's at that point that a potentially successful venture
crumbles into failure.

When you have been working 18 hours a day, seven days
a week for months, and are completely exhausted, it doesn't
take much to make you throw in the towel. Things that
wouldn't normally faze you – like an unpaid bill or your kids
complaining that they haven't seen you for days – can make
you wonder why you're working so hard, especially if the
financial rewards are yet to materialise. Every week, for
countless reasons, entrepreneurs walk away from potentially
lucrative business opportunities. You need to make sure that
you don't become one of them.

I've already suggested that one way to incentivise entrepreneurs to give their all is to put in place a financial penalty to walking away. If you stand to lose your home or be lumbered with a debt you will be unable to pay, this has the effect of increasing your appetite for success. But being financially invested isn't the only way of making sure you don't give up.

> Remember. If starting a business was easy, everyone would do it.

1. Set parameters

At the start of any venture, establish how you will measure your success. If you write down at the outset of a new venture to secure x many clients, or y many orders or z level of turnover, you can compare your expectation with reality. Maybe you'll see that you're not doing as badly as it feels. If you are not meeting any of your targets, then the chances are that walking away is exactly what you should be doing. But if you are hitting one or some of them, then hopefully you'll be encouraged to hang in there.

2. What have you learned?

Ask what you've learned since you started and see what, knowing what you do now, you'd do differently if you started all over again. It's difficult when you're starting a business to find time to reflect, but if you set aside some time to apply the things you've learned to the problems you face, you might find that things will start to get easier. Or to put it another way, if you learn something every day, then things should get better every day.

3. What have you achieved?

Look at everything you've managed to do so far. Make a list. Congratulate yourself. Next, imagine how much more you could achieve if you carried on, especially as you have already acquired so much valuable knowledge and experience.

4. Take the five-year test

Imagine it's five years from now. How much will you regret walking away? Try and picture the advice the entrepreneur you will be in five years' time would give to the entrepreneur you are now. Be your own mentor.

5. Remember this

If starting a business was easy, everyone would do it.

MISTAKE

16

Not being able to sell

THE MOST SUCCESSFUL ENTREPRENEURS – AND BY EXTENSION, the most successful businesses – have a full range of skills. They are imaginative thinkers who can also fixate on the detail; they are extroverts who could sell milk to cows and also be happy sitting alone in a room with their accounts; they are brilliant strategists who are also blessed with the communication skills to convey their strategy; they are inspirational leaders who are humble enough to recognise excellence in others. Although the best entrepreneurs have all these skills, every entrepreneur needs one above all others: the ability to sell. Everything else is secondary.

Sell your passion

Now, I am not a salesman. I do not have the gift of the gab. Half the time people can't understand my accent! You do not have to be a smooth talker with well-rehearsed patter to be able to sell, but you do have to be able to convey your passion for your business to other people. And the best – and easiest – way to feel passion for your business is by believing that your business makes the lives of others better.

When I started my first business – selling ice creams from a van – I didn't even realise I was selling, I thought I was just having a laugh with the kids who were my customers. But looking back I can see that I was absolutely passionate about my business: I was desperate for them to buy from me and not the next van, because I wanted to provide for my family. I also truly believed that my ice creams were better (the other guys didn't make smiley faces out of the strawberry sauce) and I knew that – unlike some other operators in that industry – I paid all my taxes and stuck to all the health and safety requirements. I was better than any other ice-cream seller in the area and I didn't care who knew it. That passion and belief showed itself as enthusiasm and my customers responded to it.

In my second business – operating residential care homes for the elderly – I didn't really have to sell the business to potential residents and their families because our facilities were so much better than the alternatives. In other care homes, residents were sleeping in dormitories and using commodes: we had private rooms with en suite facilities. This also made it easy to convince staff to come and work for me.

However, I did have to sell the idea of the business to the

banks from whom I needed to borrow money. To them, I probably looked like an ice-cream vendor who had got ideas above his station. But not only was I passionate about offering better care, I was utterly convinced that the business would make money and whenever a bank manager questioned me about my figures and projections, I always had the answer. My passion made me convincing, and I eventually got the money I needed.

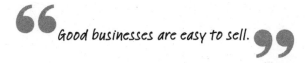

Good businesses are easy to sell.

If you truly believe in your business, if you think your service or product is better for your customers, you will be able to sell yourself and your business without feeling like a presenter on a cable TV shopping channel. Good businesses are easy to sell. Even without a patter.

This may explain why some people say they can't sell. I suspect that it's because they don't have very good businesses and deep down they know it. I was at an event recently where I met an impressive young entrepreneur who had built a fantastic website that offered free classified listings. It was a lot like *Exchange & Mart* or *Loot*, only with better functionality and better design and it was free to advertisers. He thought he was doing really well because he had about 50,000 people using his site.

'How do you make your money?' I asked, quite reasonably, 'if you don't charge people to advertise?'

He explained that it had been his business model to give away the advertising for free to encourage people to use the site but it was his intention to start charging soon. The only problem was, he'd realised he was terrified of selling. He just didn't think he could get on the phone and persuade the companies who were currently using his site to hand over their money, and he was scared that if he asked for payment online, most of his 50,000 users would simply click away. And of course, if he didn't have 50,000 users, then why would anyone bother to pay to advertise on his site when they could reach hundreds of thousands of buyers on other sites?

I think his problem was that he ultimately didn't believe in his business model. He knew that his technical and design innovations might have made his service better than that of his rivals, but they weren't enough to make anyone pay for it. I had to tell him that he didn't have a business, just a very flash website. If he really believed in his business but was still convinced he couldn't pick up the phone, he could have hired someone to sell for him, but deep down I think he knew he didn't have anything very much for an employee to sell either.

Of course, even if you do have a burning passion for your business, even if you do truly, absolutely, 100 per cent believe in it, you might still be rightly nervous about picking up the phone and selling your business. The secret to selling is to let your passion show: don't think about what you're asking for from your clients (or bank managers, or employees), focus on what you're giving them. If you know that your company can make their life easier or better, then tell them and the business will sell itself.

If you really don't think you can sell, don't try: just tell people about your business instead. A 'clear tell' is much more effective than a 'hard sell' anyway.

MISTAKE 17

If it ain't working ...

THERE'S A DEFINITION OF INSANITY – SOME PEOPLE attribute it to Albert Einstein – that goes something like this: if you do the same thing tomorrow as you did today and expect a different result, you are bonkers.

You can extend this definition to say that if you sell the same stock tomorrow as you offer for sale today and expect to sell more of it, then you're insane. Or if you expect your staff to perform differently tomorrow than they do today, then you're deluding yourself. And if you expect your customers to suddenly spend more money tomorrow than they did today; if you assume that the number of your customers will multiply overnight; if you think the same sales pitch will achieve better results – then I have to tell you that you're kidding yourself.

" *If you don't make positive changes, you shouldn't expect anyone else to change their attitude either.* "

This is genuinely a major problem with failing businesses, and it's one I see all the time. People open shops and wait for the customers to arrive. When they don't walk through the door, what do they do? They wait a little bit longer! Whether your business is online or on the high street, if you don't make changes you shouldn't expect anyone else to change their attitude towards your business.

Imagine you're in sales. You spend eight hours a day on the phone trying to get people to buy your widgets. At the end of the day, you haven't made a single sale. The next day, you get back on the phone and go through your spiel once again. 'I just need to speak to more people,' you tell yourself. Er, no, actually, you need to change what you say. Your spiel doesn't work.

Fix it!

Imagine you've just opened a shop and none of the people who walk past on the pavement pop their head through the door. What do you do? Wait to see if someone comes in tomorrow, or think about changing your window display, or perhaps stand outside and hand out leaflets?

Imagine you launched your fantastic website two months

ago and your web stats show that only 15 people have visited. Do you just sit and wait for other people to stumble across it? Of course not!

The thing about business is that if it ain't working, it ain't working for a reason – and only you can fix it. Obviously there are occasions when waiting may make a slight difference, like a retailer hanging on for a Christmas rush, but the idea that the only thing wrong with your business is that it just hasn't been in existence long enough is, well, it's crazy, isn't it?

If you aren't getting the results you hoped for, the chances are that you are doing something wrong. And that means you need to start tweaking your business – and keep tweaking it – until it connects with your customers. Because doing more of the same is a sure-fire way of making sure that your business will go under.

MISTAKE

18

Not identifying all your costs

I'VE TOUCHED ON THIS ALREADY WHEN DISCUSSING turnover and profit, but there are so many hidden costs in operating a business that I want to return to the subject in the hope that the advice here will help lots of businesses avoid some very common pitfalls.

I am a big fan of quick calculations – the kind that can fit on the back of a fag packet or a beer mat – to judge whether my BrilliantNewIdea™ stands any chance of becoming a decent business. But of course those initial calculations are incomplete and that means the margin for error in your calculations will be huge. Generally, most people overestimate the revenue potential of their business and underestimate the costs. I've found that the biggest underestimates come in the following categories:

Staff

If you pay someone a salary of £25,000 p.a., how much do you think that member of staff would actually cost you in a year? For starters you'll have to pay employer's National Insurance contributions on top of the £25k, which for most employees is currently 13.8%. Full-time employees also have a statutory entitlement to 28 days' leave a year (including bank holidays), and if that employee's work needs to be done while they're away, you'll have to pay for temporary cover which is likely to cost a minimum of one month's salary (it's frequently higher, as temporary staff usually receive higher hourly rates). If you contribute to a pension scheme, you'll have to add that to your staff costs, along with any insurance you offer to your team, like health or life cover.

Staff also come with recruitment costs. If you use a recruitment agency, you are likely to be charged a third of the staff member's first year's salary. Even if you hire in-house, there are likely to be advertising and training costs. Ongoing staff training is another hidden cost.

And now we come to other major costs of having staff – sick pay and parental leave. As an employer, you will bear the costs of statutory sick pay for staff members who are sick for more than four consecutive days. The figure for 2010/11 is around £79 a week, but if you offer more generous sick pay, then it will cost you considerably more than this. This is in addition, of course, to hiring cover for the absent staff member.

The majority of the statutory costs of maternity and paternity leave can be recouped from the government, but if your company offers more generous leave, then this will be another cost you'll have to shoulder. You may also need to recruit a replacement.

An additional expense that I've found has crept up in recent years is the cost of employment tribunals. The rise of 'no win, no fee' legal challenges has encouraged disgruntled employees to bring cases when they otherwise would not.

All in all, for every £100 I pay an employee, I have calculated that it costs me £112. So how much does an employee on £25k cost? About £28,000 p.a.

Premises

You expect to pay rent or a mortgage on your business premises, but there are so many other costs involved in having premises that you can end up in the red if you're not careful.

In addition to monthly rent payments, there may be an initial signing-on fee. This is sometimes known as a goodwill payment because it's anticipated you will retain the previous tenant's customers. You will also have rates to pay, utility bills, buildings and contents insurance and, of course, office maintenance fees. You will also need Public Liability Insurance in case your staff or your customers have an accident on your premises. And there might also be costs in meeting health and safety requirements. You'll probably also need a budget for cleaning, tea bags, loo rolls and all the other incidentals your staff and clients will expect.

Fees

You'll almost certainly need the services of a lawyer at some point in your business career, and we all know that they don't come cheap. You might also need an accountant to help with your returns or your payroll. And unlike domestic customers who are used to free banking, as a commercial customer you will have to get used to being charged for everything from depositing a cheque to arrangement fees for loans.

In my experience, professional services are often quoted by the hour, or as a percentage of the overall job. When a lawyer or an architect has the option of advertising their services as costing £150 an hour or 6 per cent, they usually go for the latter as it sounds more reasonable. Either way, when they bill you for a hundred hours' work, or for a percentage of a six-figure invoice, you can get badly stung. My advice is to *always fix your fees*. Agree a price in advance for the total service, and then agree to a cap on any expenses they can charge.

Finance

As well as arrangement fees, banks and finance companies will also charge you interest on any money you borrow. So if you borrow £100,000 to buy some new equipment at a rate of 8 per cent per annum and pay it back over three years, you will end up paying something like £116,000 (this is because your interest in Year 1 will be around £8k, but decrease in Years 2 and 3 as you repay the capital amount). If you've only budgeted for £100k, you're going to find yourself with a £16k deficit. So whenever you take out a loan, ask your lender for the total amount payable and check that you really can afford the repayments.

You also need to establish whether you are borrowing on a fixed or variable rate of interest. If you are on the latter and interest rates start to rise, will you be able to meet your repayments? If you need certainty, you might be better off on a fixed rate, though this will inevitably mean an arrangement fee.

Technology

Computer systems have a way of costing an awful lot more than you anticipate. You might look at the PC World website and think you know the cost of buying a computer, but trust me, we're talking tips and icebergs. There's maintenance, software, firewalls, back-up servers, printers (and toner cartridges), networking and that's before we get to built-in obsolescence and the fact that fancy bits of kit sometimes go home with the staff. If you need bespoke software designed for you, you might also need a stiff drink.

Non-payment

Your budgets should also allow for a proportion of non-payment by your clients. Some people will always try and pay their bills late, in instalments or not at all. I now employ two people full time to chase our non-payers, but there will always be a tiny percentage of people who will never pay because they've gone bankrupt, moved abroad or died. If you operate on narrow margins, not knowing your non-payment rates could be catastrophic for your business.

Contingency costs

Pretty much everything in business costs more than you think it will. Building projects – whether it's websites or bricks and mortar – almost always overrun. If you have fixed your costs and have a watertight contract, you will be insulated from the worst of the overspend, but if you were planning to start using a building or a website on a certain date and it's not ready, then this will still cause your business financial pain. Whatever your project, whatever your budget, you should always include a contingency allowance: I suggest this should be a minimum of 10 per cent of the total spend. You might find 25 per cent is more realistic.

Emergencies

When I ran my ice-cream business, no matter how tight things got, I always kept a few hundred quid to one side. I knew I needed that money just in case my van broke down or something else unforeseen happened. No van, no business, no income. I could do most repairs myself – I had trained as a fitter and welder when I was younger – but if I couldn't fix it, I had to know that I could get the garage to fix it straight away.

One day I was involved in an accident. The damage was too much for me to repair on my own, and there was no way I could wait around for the insurance to pay up. That's when my emergency fund saved my business. I was back on the road in days rather than weeks.

Think about the emergencies that would bring your business to a halt, and then think how much money you need to have in a rainy-day fund just in case the worst happens.

MISTAKE

19

Being flattered by turnover

ONE OF MY FAVOURITE BUSINESS PHRASES IS THAT 'turnover is vanity and profit is sanity'. I've seen so many people over the years allow themselves to be flattered by their revenue, only to be humiliated by their profit.

The difference between turnover and profit

Before I go any further, I'd better spell out the difference between turnover and profit. Turnover is all the money your business has coming in, and profit is the money you have left from your turnover once you've paid all your bills.

It helps some people to think about the two in terms of a salary. Someone on a salary of £30,000 a year has an annual turnover of £30,000, but once they've paid their tax, national insurance, bills, their shopping and entertainment, their rent and train fares they might be lucky if they're left with £100 a month. That's their profit. Their annual profit – i.e., money they could put into a savings account – would be £1,200. Or put it another way, 4 per cent.

> **If you don't know the difference between revenue and profit, the scale of your ignorance is enormous.**

The difference between turnover and profit is often similar in business. Bannatyne Fitness Group has a turnover of around £100 million a year, and our profit before interest and tax after costs is around £28 million. Once we've paid tax on those profits and made the repayments on our loans, we are left with around £2m a year. It should be clear from these figures that if you don't know the difference between revenue and profit, the magnitude of your ignorance is enormous.

It is perfectly possible for a business with a multi-million-pound turnover to go bust. Look at Woolworths, or Enron or Barings Bank – these were all businesses with massive amounts of money on their balance sheets, but as soon as the money came in, it went straight back out again. You could also look at the UK Government's books. It raises billions through taxation, but it still has to borrow more each year because the nation is spending more than it earns.

It has been my experience that when company owners talk about their turnover it's because they're too embarrassed to talk about their profit. Companies are valued on their profit, not their turnover, and ultimately it doesn't matter how big your turnover is if it isn't any larger than your costs.

I understand why people talk about their turnover: it's the business equivalent of bragging about how big your house is without revealing the enormous size of your mortgage. And there is also an assumption among the general public that a company with a turnover of several millions 'must be doing well'. It's fine to brag about your turnover to others, but it's important that in private you acknowledge the size of your profit.

Part of the problem comes from the fact that many entre-preneurs aren't actually all that good with figures. If that's you, I would ask you to turn back to the chapter on taking responsibility for everything your business does. If you rely on an accountant to tell you what your figures are, then you're not taking sufficient responsibility for them. In my experience, the kind of entrepreneur who doesn't take responsibility for their own figures, also tends to be the kind of person who only likes to hear good news. When their accountant tells them an impressive turnover figure they stop listening before the less-than-impressive profit figure is revealed!

Keeping on top on your costs

However, even those entrepreneurs who are on top of their accounts still manage to miscalculate their profit and this is generally because they haven't properly identified all their costs. If you're operating with a small profit margin, knowing all your costs in detail is absolutely vital. A 'back-of-the-fag-packet' calculation is a great tool when you're developing a business idea, but when you are operational, there is no room for generalisations and assumptions. The best way to get an accurate figure for your costs is to keep all receipts and to patiently go through them. Just as with your bills at home, it's very easy to forget incidental expenditure. Most of us can estimate fairly accurately how much we spend on a weekly supermarket shop, but often it's the unplanned convenience purchases and take-away dinners that send domestic accounts into the red. Businesses have those sorts of incidental purchases too. Whether it's ordering too many taxis or spending more on sick cover than you had anticipated, those extra £10 and £100 purchases can add up to a significant figure.

I realise that income is far more exciting to an entrepreneur than expenditure, but if you are not on top of your spending, then you have no idea what your profit is.

Case study 3: Motorola

In 1990 mobile phones were so big that most people didn't even bother to carry them around. They were known as carphones because they were too big for pockets and handbags. That wasn't the only problem with early mobiles: reception was terrible. It was OK if you were in London, but if you left the capital – even going to Manchester or Newcastle – you couldn't be sure you'd be able to get a signal. The idea of one day being able to use your mobile phone while yachting off the coast of Cap d'Antibes was just preposterous.

Motorola had the answer: satellite phones. Instead of ramping up the roll-out of mobile phone masts, Motorola had the idea to do away with the mast network altogether. In what must be one of the most ambitious business plans ever written, Motorola set out to a) buy a fleet of rockets from the Russians, the Americans and the Chinese, b) manufacture 72 satellites, c) use 'a' to launch 'b' into orbit, and d) build a global network of satellite receiving stations. This would enable them to offer global coverage to phone users whether they were in an Antarctic research station or on a camel ride across the Sahara. No other phone company would be able to compete and they would be assured of global dominance.

Motorola's was a meticulously well-laid plan. Something that technologically complex had to be. And the costs were so enormous that each stage had to be rigorously tested before they moved on to the next level. Motorola called its new phone Iridium and launched it as a separate company. Before a single Iridium phone had been bought, it had taken eight years and cost $5.2 billion dollars. Yes, billion. *But within a year of the first Iridium call being made in 1998, the company had filed for bankruptcy.*

The problem with Iridium wasn't so much that their phones cost $3,000 each, or that you couldn't make calls from inside a car or a building because you had to have a direct line of sight to a satellite. Nor was it that their per-minute charges were in dollars rather than cents. The main issue was that Motorola had launched a 1990 business in 1998. In the eight years between launching Iridium the company and Iridium the phone, the market had changed radically. In the intervening years, a network of phone masts had been built and it had become quite rare to find yourself out of range. The size of mobile phones had also shrunk, as had the cost of making a call. Unless you really did need to make a call while riding a camel across the desert or trekking to the South Pole, why would you pay $7 per minute to make a call when you could pay 7 cents with a regular mobile phone?

Iridium's 1990 business plan had predicted it would win 42 million customers worldwide. At its peak it had just 30,000 subscribers. The business went into administration and the business's satellite network was bought from the receivers for $25 million, approximately half a per cent of what it had cost to build. You can still buy an Iridium phone (for about £1,000) and it seems there are enough people who regularly ride camels across deserts to keep the new company in business. It's a niche, specialist business but it is profitable, unlike its predecessor, which must go down in history as one of the most expensive start-up business failures in history.

The really incredible thing about this story is that, at some point in Iridium's development, you just know that one member of the team called up another member of the team using a mobile phone. A regular one that relied on the mast network. They probably had a really long conversation about some technical aspect of Iridium and it didn't even occur to them that the product they were *discussing was already obsolete because of the product they were using! Surely someone, at some point, would have said: 'You know what, guys, I think maybe we missed the boat on this one. What do you say we cut our losses?' It would seem not.*

MISTAKE

20

Not understanding cashflow

> *If you don't know your cashflow, you don't know your business.*

THIS IS ONE OF THE MOST IMPORTANT CHAPTERS IN this book. If you don't know your cashflow, you don't know your business. What many inexperienced entrepreneurs fail to realise until it's too late is that it is perfectly possible for a profitable business to run out of cash.

Cashflow is particularly relevant for businesses with seasonal income. In certain types of agriculture, for example, the majority of the year's money is earned at the time of harvest. In the hotel and holiday business, earnings are at their highest in summer, with spikes at half-term and school holidays. Florists make a huge portion of their profits on just two days of the year – Valentine's Day and Mother's Day – while jewellery retailers can make as much as half their income in December.

There are several scenarios in which a decent business with decent earnings can discover the money cupboard is bare. The most common one is the start-up business that has upfront costs before any revenue is produced, and in this situation most entrepreneurs realise they need start-up capital to get them to the profitable months. They understand that over the months they can gradually increase their turnover and start to pay down their debt; when the debt is cleared, they will have enough cash to invest in their business and grow it. But it's not just at the start of a business that your costs can dwarf your revenues, and that's when businesses often find themselves in trouble.

In business, we usually talk about annual turnover and year-end profits, which would be absolutely fine if we didn't pay our bills monthly. Those annual figures hide the pain that bad cashflow can inflict on your business. Let me show you: here's an example of a mythical business with regular revenues and regular costs:

Company A

	Jan	Feb	Mar	Apr	May	Jun
Revenue (£)	10,000	10,000	10,000	10,000	10,000	10,000
Costs (£)	7,000	7,000	7,000	7,000	7,000	7,000
Profit (£)	3,000	3,000	3,000	3,000	3,000	3,000

	Jul	Aug	Sep	Oct	Nov	Dec
Revenue (£)	10,000	10,000	10,000	10,000	10,000	10,000
Costs (£)	7,000	7,000	7,000	7,000	7,000	7,000
Profit (£)	3,000	3,000	3,000	3,000	3,000	3,000

Annual profit (£)   36,000

As I say, this is a mythical business, which is why its costs and revenues never fluctuate. In reality, revenues and costs are never the same every month. In the next example, the overall revenue and costs are the same, but there are potentially tricky monthly fluctuations:

Company B

	Jan	Feb	Mar	Apr	May	Jun
Revenue (£)	10,000	10,000	5,000	10,000	12,500	10,000
Costs (£)	12,000	10,000	7,000	7,000	7,000	10,000
Profit (£)	-2,000	0	-2,000	3,000	5,500	0

	Jul	Aug	Sep	Oct	Nov	Dec
Revenue (£)	7,500	10,000	10,000	10,000	10,000	15,000
Costs (£)	7,000	4,000	4,000	2,000	7,000	7,000
Profit (£)	500	6,000	6,000	8,000	3,000	8,000

Annual profit (£)   36,000

Company A and Company B both produce an annual turnover of £36,000, but in January and March, Company B goes into the red. Its cashflow problem is actually a little worse than it looks on paper: it doesn't just need a buffer of £2,000 – either through a loan or an investment – it needs £4,000 because January's loss will be carried forward into February, and as it only breaks even in February, that £2,000 deficit is carried through until March where it becomes a £4,000 debt. If all of April's profit is used to pay down that debt, the business still owes £1,000 which won't be paid back for another month.

A and B have the same revenue and the same profit, but completely different cashflow issues. Now let's take a look at Company C:

Company C

	Jan	Feb	Mar	Apr	May	Jun
Revenue (£)	10,000	10,000	10,000	10,000	10,000	10,000
Costs (£)	7,000	7,000	7,000	7,000	7,000	7,000
Profit (£)	3,000	3,000	3,000	3,000	3,000	3,000

	Jul	Aug	Sep	Oct	Nov	Dec
Revenue (£)	10,000	10,000	10,000	10,000	10,000	10,000
Costs (£)	7,000	7,000	7,000	25,000	7,000	7,000
Profit (£)	3,000	3,000	3,000	-15,000	3,000	3,000

Annual profit (£)	18,000

This is identical to Company A except for October when Company C gets hit by a one-off expense. If you look at the year-end figure, this business still makes a profit, but if the monthly profits haven't been put to one side, this business won't be able to pay its bills at the end of the year.

Another way a profitable business can have cashflow problems is when its assets are added to its balance sheet. When year-end accounts are produced, as well as listing revenues and costs, it's usual practice to add in the value of any assets the company holds, the most common of which is stock. Let me give you an example: if a company has revenues of £850,000 and costs of £1,000,000, you might expect its accounts to show a £150,000 loss. But if that company also has £200,000 worth of stock, that asset is added to the balance sheet and would create a £50,000 profit. This mistake is compounded when the valuation of those assets is wrong. I came across a great example of this when I worked on a TV show called *Mind Your Own Business* where I helped struggling entrepreneurs get out of a hole. I spent an episode with a woman who ran a clothing boutique whose accounts were much healthier than her till receipts. I soon found out this was because she was keeping her stock – at the original selling price – on her books as an asset. Of course, in the world of fashion, last year's stock is pretty much worthless. I had to tell this woman that she was kidding herself if she thought her paper profit would ever be converted into cash.

VAT can also cause problems for new entrepreneurs as it is something that is paid quarterly. If your turnover is in excess of £70,000 you must be registered for VAT by law. This means that – for most industries and sectors – you must charge your customers 20 per cent VAT. What you are effectively doing is collecting a tax on behalf of HMRC, because every three months you have to hand over that 20 per cent – less any VAT you've paid on goods and services you've bought in – to the government. So for three months, you might look at your bank balance and think you're doing better than you thought, and then suddenly see a big drop in your bank balance when the VAT demand gets paid.

Collecting VAT can be a big help to your business as it is effectively a short-term interest-free loan from the government. You get 20 per cent more money coming through your tills, which might enable you to pay other bills or invest in the business. So long as you remember that the money will quickly become due, you won't have a problem. But if you spend it like it's yours to keep, your cashflow can quickly dive into the red.

The best way to make sure you don't run into problems with your cashflow is to accurately forecast your income and expenditure. Instead of rounding things up – fag-packet style – into annual figures, work through your likely costs and earnings month by month. If you can see you'll earn most of your money in the run-up to Christmas, then you need to be disciplined about putting the surplus to one side to prop up your balance sheet for the rest of the year. If you can anticipate that you will incur costs at a certain time of year, then you can budget for them and set money aside in advance. If that isn't possible, you can ensure you've got lending in place to cover a shortfall.

If you do hit the cashflow buffers, I have one piece of good news. Investors love businesses with cashflow problems. It offers them the chance to put their money into an otherwise sound investment. And they get to invest at a point when the business is so distressed its owners will be prepared to give away a larger percentage of the equity than they would if there wasn't an immediate threat of going bust! Every cloud . . .

MISTAKE 21

The Extrapolation Trap

The Gaboom story

In series 8 of *Dragons' Den*, a bright young woman called Jessica Radcliffe came to pitch her games-swapping service Gaboom.co.uk. Gaboom lets gamers swap games they have for games they want with other players. At the time, she told us, no one else in the UK was offering such a service, but it was difficult to see how Gaboom would make money; after all, swapping intrinsically means that no cash changes hands. Jessica – whose presentation was of a very high calibre – explained that Gaboom made money on the postage of the games. It wasn't a lot on each transaction, but if the site had millions of users then those micro fees would start to add up. At this point, I think it was fair to say that all five Dragons were potentially interested in investing not just in Jessica, but also in Gaboom.

Then Jessica told us about Gaboom's other income stream: for a small fee of a couple of quid, Gaboom would quality assure the swapped games. It sounded like a fantastic service for someone who wants the reassurance the game they will receive works properly, but as a business model it was utterly implausible. If a couple of customers want their game checked, you could probably fit the checking in around other tasks, but if Gaboom took off and thousands of people wanted their games checked, then Gaboom would grind to a halt. First they have to collect the post, then open the post, then check the game, then repackage the game. How long would that take? Half an hour? Even if it's only 20 minutes, Gaboom was only charging a few quid for this service, which means the income per member of staff wouldn't be much more than the minimum wage, and once other costs had been deducted, there would hardly be anything left.

Now let's say that Gaboom got 100 games a day to check, at three per hour, they would need at least four members of staff each working an eight-hour day just to check and pack the games. If they got 1,000 games a day, they would need 40 members of staff, and that would mean bigger premises, bigger overheads, bigger risks – and that would probably be enough to wipe out the tiny profit as there are no significant economies of scale when each game needs to be checked by a human being. It was at this point in Jessica's presentation that Gaboom tripped and fell slap bang into the Extrapolation Trap.

A classic mistake

The Extrapolation Trap is a classic mistake made by inexperienced entrepreneurs when they write their business plans.

They assume that a business that works well on a small scale will work equally well on a larger scale. I completely understand why; after all, if a business makes money doing something, why wouldn't it make more money doing more of the same?

I was recently sent a business plan by a young company seeking investment. Their business offered online news and gossip for different industries. They already had a site aimed at people who worked in the media and had plans to roll out their service to other industries. If I invested, they told me they would launch a site for bankers, then one for the oil industry, then one for people in fashion and so on. As well as making money from subscriptions to their websites, they were also going to offer networking events for each industry. Their aim was to start a new service for a new industry every two months. And not just in the UK, but in the United States, Australia and a few other territories too: after all, these are international industries.

It wasn't the worst business plan I'd ever seen, but it is one of the best examples of the Extrapolation Trap I've ever come across. In two years' time, their business plan promised to have launched 12 services in the UK, and a slightly smaller number in each of their overseas territories. In total, they would have over 50 different websites targeting different industries in different countries, and each of them would hold a networking event each month.

'Is it really plausible,' I asked the founders at the end of their presentation to me, 'that in just two years' time you will be organising events at such a level that you'll be doing more than one a day?' I'm often asked to speak at events and I have some idea of how much work they take to organise. 'I don't think you can do it. I'd be surprised if anyone can do it.'

What had seemed plausible at a small scale – a boutique news service for individual industries married with regular events – seemed utterly ridiculous when extrapolated every few months to its (il)logical conclusion.

The Extrapolation Trap can be a particularly nasty pitfall if you are planning your business with the help of a spreadsheet. Spreadsheets let you 'model' your business by fiddling with formulae to judge how much and how quickly a business will grow. Spreadsheets are fantastically helpful tools when you're working out the potential of your business. They can help you forecast how much investment you will need, what profit you stand to make and when you will break even. But they also allow you to scale up your business without applying common sense. Without really noticing, modest formulae predicting a 30 per cent, or even 100 per cent, growth turn your plausible business into a joke.

The truth is, most businesses find their natural size.

When inexperienced entrepreneurs start playing around with spreadsheets, they assume that if the original costs and figures are accurate and the projected rate of growth is accurate, then the eventual size of their business must be plausible. It's often only when they use these 'plausible' projections to find investment that an investor will point out the flaws. The truth is, most businesses find their natural size and they can't all easily or sensibly become international conglomerates. For

Gaboom, that size was as a boutique site for avid gamers, not a multimillion-pound venture. For Bannatyne Fitness, for example, we're probably near our optimum size. We can't keep opening new health clubs at the same rate every year as there just aren't that many towns and cities to support an infinite number of clubs.

How to avoid the Extrapolation Trap

The good news is that it is very, very easy to avoid the Extrapolation Trap. All you have to do is look at the size you predict your business will grow to and ask some pretty simple questions:

- How many staff will that take?

- Where will those staff work?

- Are there actually enough customers for this product/ service?

- Am I capable of running that kind of business?

- If I were an investor, would I think this plan was credible?

These are not the kinds of questions you need expensive business analysts to answer. You probably just need to ask your gran; and if she thinks your planning is a bit ambitious, then it almost certainly is.

MISTAKE

22

Not doing a sensitivity analysis

What is it?

I confess that when I first started out in business I had never heard of a sensitivity analysis. Now that I do know about it, I wouldn't want to be without it. A sensitivity analysis is one of the best defences a business can have against going under because it is a really simple tool that lets you understand how robust your business is.

To carry out a sensitivity analysis you just need a set of your business's accounts and all you do is play around with your costs and revenues. Simply ask yourself how far your costs could rise before you'd end up in the red: 10, 20, 50 per cent? And then see how far your revenues could fall before you couldn't pay your bills: 5, 15, 25 per cent?

The sensitivity analysis is particularly useful if your business is heavily geared – i.e., you have a lot of debt – you can be particularly vulnerable to changes in bank lending rates. Your loan repayments could well be your business's biggest cost, which means a 1 per cent rate rise could hurt your profit margin by a lot more than 1 per cent. It doesn't sound a lot, but I know from my own businesses how much 1 per cent impacts the bottom line.

In 2011, the VAT rate increased from 17.5 to 20 per cent. The 2.5 per cent difference might not sound like very much, but on Bannatyne Fitness's turnover of £100 million, it actually meant we were handing over an extra £2.5 million in tax each year because we didn't feel we could pass on the increase to our members. It might have been a small percentage, but it translated into a huge amount of money.

1. It gives you a reality check

When we look at our accounts we are looking at actual figures that correspond with actual pounds. If the figure is big enough, we tend to feel pretty secure. But if your £1 million profit is made on a tiny margin, you can easily see that a small percentage shift could wipe out a massive chunk of your earnings – or wipe the business out altogether. If you know all that's standing between you and your millions is a 5 per cent cushion, you might behave rather differently than if it were 50 per cent.

> **66** *A sensitivity analysis can be your wake-up call to danger.* **99**

2. It can trigger the smoke alarm

Just as a smoke alarm wakes you up in the night to give you a better chance of escaping a fire, so a sensitivity analysis can be your wake-up call to danger for your business. If you know you can only let revenues dip by 20 per cent, then when they start to slide, you can make adjustments and preparations. As soon as revenues slip, you can begin to cut costs. Or if costs start to rise, you can take evasive action to prevent them eating too far into your profits.

3. It gives you confidence

If you know your business can survive a 10 per cent drop in revenue, then you're not going to panic when your income drops by 5 per cent. As long as the financial reality stays within the margins you've identified, you can continue to operate with confidence.

How useful is it?

When you perform a sensitivity analysis you need to look at each area of expenditure and income separately. You might be able to absorb a 50 per cent hike in some costs, while a 5 per cent increase in other costs could wipe you out. The more detail you put into your sensitivity analysis, the more useful it will be.

Since I discovered the wonders of the sensitivity analysis, I've realised how valuable it is as it helps me make better decisions. In case you're interested, in my businesses I am always looking for a 40 per cent cushion. I know that my overall costs can rise by 20 per cent at the same time as my revenues drop by 20 per cent and still be able to stay afloat. The wider the margin your sensitivity analysis reveals, the more likely it is your business will endure. If you fail to do a sensitivity analysis, then you are failing to protect your venture.

MISTAKE

23

Making a poor first impression

Don't compound your initial error

Imagine you and a friend decide to try out a new restaurant. You've heard good things about it in the papers and it's run by a chef who used to work somewhere you've previously had good food.

When you walk in, the décor is pleasant enough, but none of the staff acknowledge your arrival. The two of you stand near the door for a few minutes waiting for someone to show you to your table. It's not a terrible start, but it's hardly a brilliant beginning to a night out. Already you're thinking that it's not as good as you'd hoped it might be.

When the food comes, there's something wrong with it. The meat is fatty, the potatoes are cold and the gravy is missing. It doesn't matter that the vegetables are fantastic. You and your mate start to size up each other's meal. 'It's very tasty, but . . .' The more you eat of your meal, the more you realise just how much of the joint is fat and gristle but it's too late to send it back. 'The chef,' you say to your guest, 'shouldn't let a meal go out like this. He must have known the joint was fatty.'

When the waiter collects your plates, you point to the pile of fat and say that you don't think it's acceptable. You don't even get round to telling him about the potatoes and gravy. 'I'll let the chef know,' the waiter promises.

The waiter has just compounded the chef's mistake. Immediately he should have offered to bring you another meal or said that there wouldn't be a charge for your main course. Instead he comes back a few minutes later to say that the chef has apologised and that they'd like to offer you a free coffee.

Coffee? Coffee! It should be a free dessert at least.

It doesn't really matter what happens after this because that restaurant has probably lost your custom for good. It's not that the food was absolutely awful or the service was truly terrible, but when there are other restaurants to choose from, why on earth would you go back? The chef and the manager might be thinking, 'Well they ate most of it, they must have enjoyed it.' It's even possible you might leave a tip in this situation because the waiter wasn't at fault. The management have no reason to realise that they've probably lost your custom *for ever*.

If it were me, the service would have had to be charming, the bill slashed in half or the manager insisting that we returned in a week for a free bottle of wine to give it another chance. Other than that, only a sign saying 'Under New Management' would make me go back.

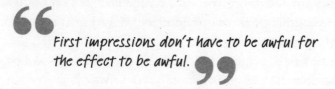

> *First impressions don't have to be awful for the effect to be awful.*

First impressions don't have to be awful for the effect on your business to be awful. If you deliver goods late, in less-than-perfect condition or you get the order wrong you give customers the opportunity to walk away. Remember the DeLorean car company? It never recovered from initial reviews of its DMC-12 that listed a string of minor faults. It became known as a faulty car and its reputation stuck.

What's particularly cruel is that if your service is just a bit rubbish, rather than absolutely awful, you may never know why customers don't come back. If, going back to the restaurant example, you had had a truly terrible meal, you would have asked to see the manager, or written a letter of complaint, and that way the owner could learn and make changes. If you simply disappoint your customers, they drift away and you never know why. And as customer acquisition is just about the hardest thing to do in business, a company that squanders new customers won't survive for long.

Established businesses with impressive track records and long-standing relationships with their customers can usually weather a rocky patch, but new businesses aren't cut any slack. Your service, your prices and your goods have to be of a very high standard to get repeat business: you have to give customers a reason to keep on using your company. If inexperienced entrepreneurs think their customers will make allowances for their shortcomings because they're new, they are very, very mistaken. If anything, you have to exceed your customers' expectations to succeed.

So how can you make sure you always make a good first impression? The simplest and most effective way is just to put yourself in your customer's shoes. Think about how they will interact with your company. How would you like the phone to be answered if you were a customer? How promptly would you want your goods delivered? Would you like to be served with a smile? What condition would you like your goods to be in?

Managing expectations

It's really not very hard to work out what will make potential customers respond positively to your new business, and if you exceed their expectations, they may be more willing to put up with the odd lapse in service later on. If you don't think you are geared up to offer the kind of service that you think your customers will expect, then maybe you should think about delaying your launch until you are up to the job. Better to lose a week's takings at the beginning than to be condemned to shutting for good because you rushed your launch. Make sure your premises are ready, your systems are tested and your staff are trained.

The other option you have is to reduce people's expectations. In the theatre, productions often have a week of preview performances before the opening night. The previews are often less than half the usual ticket price and the audience knows that the actors might fluff the odd line, and the lighting director might leave the stage in darkness, but the audience doesn't mind because they're not expecting everything to be perfect. I think other industries could learn from this. If a new restaurant offered half-price meals for the first week, they'd probably get enough people through the door to really test the kitchen and waiting staff and the customers would tolerate the odd cold potato.

There are two really important points to make about first impressions:

1 *It doesn't have to be awful to be awful.* You might think you've offered a reasonable service, but if it was below what your customer had a right to expect, they will be very unlikely to use you again.

2 *If you mess up, you 'fess up.* If you know your business has let your customers down, then it's up to you to make amends. Let your customers know – in person, by phone, by sending them a free gift – that you've fallen short of their expectations and offer them an incentive to use you again.

First impressions have always been important, but now that businesses are reviewed and rated online, a disgruntled customer can have a disproportionate effect on your business. A bad review stays on forums and review sites for ever and you'll need a lot of five-star reviews to offset the impact of any one-star write-ups. It's a cliché but it's still true: you never get a second chance to make a first impression. Businesses can be made or broken in the first week of trading.

MISTAKE

24

The 1 per cent gambit

WHEN YOU'VE BEEN INVESTING IN BUSINESSES FOR AS long as I have, you develop an intuition about who's going to make it. I know other investors can be put off by a sloppy dresser, or a weak handshake, or a boast that an investment is a 'once in a lifetime' opportunity to make millions – it never, ever is – but I've got my own list of things an entrepreneur can say or do that will ensure I will not invest in them. These tics and flaws are like early warning radar to alert me that a project and its founder are doomed to failure.

It took a couple of series of *Dragons' Den* for me to completely hone my armoury of early warning triggers, but one phrase came up so often in unsuccessful presentations that I quickly realised it was a very accurate indicator of an entrepreneur who doesn't know what they're doing. Top of that list is the 1 per cent gambit, which works like this:

66 *It's an accurate indicator that someone doesn't know what they're doing.* 99

The entrepreneur starts their presentation by telling us about the industry they work in. This is a very good start: as investors, we can't know about every industry, so giving us a bit of background is really useful. They then say something like: 'The global widget market is worth £250 million and if we only capture 1 per cent of that market we stand to deliver returns of [insert your own unrealistic figure here] in two years' time.'

I have come to realise that anyone who says they only need or want or are aiming for just 1 per cent of the market has no idea *whatsoever* about the realities of business. If you've ever been in a meeting with a sales rep who says 'and we only need 1 per cent of our existing customers to buy our new product', met a website owner who says 'and we only need 1 per cent of our visitors to click on the link' or heard any other variation of the 1 per cent gambit, then you've witnessed one of the all-time classic business mistakes.

There are so many reasons why this is such a good indicator of a bad entrepreneur. For starters, there seems to be an assumption that such a modest ambition must be easy to achieve. It's almost as if they think every business that launches is automatically entitled to at least 1 per cent of the global market. You'd have to be rubbish not to even get a measly 1 per cent, right? In my experience, if someone thinks something is going to be easy, then they aren't expecting to work hard for it, nor do they see the need to make the necessary plans to get that 1 per cent. What they don't realise is that saying they're going to get 1 per cent of the market is actually as ridiculous as them saying they're going to get 10 per cent. In fact, I might actually take someone aiming for 10 per cent more seriously, because it probably means they have given their plans more careful consideration.

The 1 per cent gambit becomes even more meaningless when you ask entrepreneurs *which* market they are hoping to get a slice of: the baby market, the pram market, the luxury pram market, the budget pram market, the UK market or the EU market? Markets aren't easily defined.

What really matters

What very few people seem to realise is that it's not *market share* that matters, it's *market*. As an investor, I want to know if you've identified your customers, that you understand them and that you've found out how to reach them. It doesn't matter whether you end up with 0.5 per cent of the market or over 50 per cent; what matters is that your figures add up and that you can reach enough customers to get you to profit and keep you there.

So if you ever hear yourself falling back on the 1 per cent gambit, please have a word with yourself and go straight back to the drawing board.

MISTAKE

25

Listening to your mum

I AM REALLY SORRY TO BE THE ONE TO BREAK THIS TO you. You might want to sit down. The thing is, well, I should really just come right out and say it: your mum is a liar. What makes it worse is that she doesn't lie to everyone: she only lies to you. Your mum thinks you are smarter than you are. She thinks you are better-looking than you are. And she thinks your idea for a business is way, way better than it actually is.

It has been my experience that when someone tries to persuade me that their ridiculous venture is TheNextBig Thing™ when it is patently TheWorstIdeaEver™, their reason for pursuing the venture with confidence stems from the fact that 'my mum thought it was a really great idea,' or because 'my mum said she would buy one.'

Saying that your mum thinks your business is a winner is just as bad as telling me you only want 1 per cent of the market. It is one of the stupidest things an entrepreneur can say, and if you ever utter those words, you should wash your mouth out with soap!

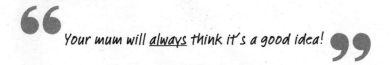

Your mum will always think it's a good idea!

Let me tell you straight: your mum will always think it's a good idea. It's what the rest of the world thinks that matters. Even if – and I mean this – your mum is the target market for your business. Ask some other people what they think. Stand in the street and take a survey. Poll opinions in Facebook. Ask anyone other than your mum (except favourite aunts, jolly uncles, doting grandparents etc. etc.).

26

Writing a business plan backwards

Who your business plan is really for

Most people who start a business write some kind of business plan. I always recommend that you write a business plan, even if you're a very experienced entrepreneur, and even if your business is very straightforward.

> A good business plan helps you understand your business better and makes you solve problems before they arise.

A business plan should map out a likely future for a new venture. It should set out why you're starting the business, what the business does and why it will be successful. Many people think that business plans are just documents to impress bank managers with, or to woo investors with, but the very best business plans are written for the business founders themselves. Yes, I said *for*, not *by*. That's because a good business plan helps you understand your business better and makes you solve problems before they've arisen.

The best business plans identify what the business does, how it will make money, where the market is and how the market will be reached. It will then map out plans for future expansion and predict costs and revenues to give an outline of the future shape of the business. The process of writing a business plan should help you get to know your business inside out and act as a reliable road map through the crazy months that follow the launch of any new enterprise. The problem arises when people write their maps backwards.

Forwards, not backwards

Instead of building up their business model by looking at the size of the market, gauging the appetite for the new product or service and assessing the likely costs in reaching customers, some entrepreneurs start by working out how much money they need to make and work backwards from there. Let's be absolutely clear about this: you cannot make the figures fit the business, you have to let the business form the figures.

Some entrepreneurs think about the salaries they'd like to earn, the offices they'd like to work in and the cars they'd like to drive, and build up a picture of a business that is very expensive to run. Those expenses mean they have to sell more of whatever it is their business sells, and so they create a business plan that predicts very high sales figures that bear absolutely no relation to the market. What they're doing is the equivalent of wanting to buy a very expensive house and getting a mortgage for it on the fraudulent basis of saying they earn a very high salary when they have no income at all.

I understand why some people choose to write their business plans backwards. They need to borrow money or get investment at a certain level and they think the only way they can do this is if they produce the most amazing predictions. Their fraud is compounded by the fact that business plans have near-magical abilities to look like they make sense when they don't. Suddenly, as soon as something is written down in black and white, it seems real, it seems plausible, it seems *believable*. And that's where the real trouble lies: people start to think their own fabrications will come true. And that makes it easier for them to convince other people about their venture. Sadly, some investors – usually referred to as family, friends and fools – are conned by their impressive forecasts and subsequently lose their money.

The biggest loss I ever made in business was in a company called Lady In Leisure, a small group of women-only gyms that I tried to buy in the mid-1990s. It was a badly run business and I saw an opportunity to make changes – and make a profit. I started buying shares in the company, but before I could take control, the business went into administration and the shares I had spent just over £1 million on were suddenly worthless. It was only afterwards when I was able to see all the paperwork that I realised why the business had been so badly run: it had been based on a backwards business plan. Well, several plans actually. The founders wrote their initial plan to show that their profits would be sufficient to pay off their loans. When costs overran, their response wasn't to find ways to reduce their costs or increase their profits, it looked like they simply rewrote their business plan to show a projection for increased profits, and so the banks lent them even more money!

If you're ever tempted to write your plan backwards, remember this: a brilliant business plan rarely makes a brilliant business. A good plan, however, usually helps you build a good business.

Case study 4: Hoover

Speak to most people who work in marketing and they'll tell you that if they were to get a 5 per cent response to any campaign they would be delighted. What that means is that if you send out 100 leaflets, five people get in touch. An average response rate to most marketing campaigns would be 2 or 3 per cent. If you keep that in mind, you can just about comprehend how Hoover made the biggest marketing mistake of all time.

In 1992, when some bright spark in their UK office suggested offering free flights to customers who spent over £100 on their appliances, the other people round the table probably thought the offer would tempt lots of customers to buy products with only a handful taking up the free offer. What did they have to lose? About £50 million, as it turned out.

Take Hoover's iconic vacuum cleaners as an example. I don't know what the profit margin is on your average vacuum cleaner, but of every £100 spent in stores on Hoover products, I reckon about £35 went to the store. How much does it cost to make a vacuum cleaner? Let's say that the cost to Hoover in 1992 was £20. That meant their gross profit on a £100 vacuum cleaner was £45. It was out of that profit that Hoover had to procure the flights for customers. Keep in mind that this was before the days of Ryanair and other budget airlines. Nevertheless, those marketing folk at Hoover thought it was a good idea.

Initially, the offer was for two return flights in Europe and the promotion was so effective at shifting a backlog of Hoover products that the company decided to expand the offer: two free flights to the US. They thought it would be enough to empty their warehouse of old stock. Their tagline for the campaign was 'Two return seats: unbelievable'.

Yet, because that's what it said on the tags on their products their customers had every right believe them. Sure there was some small print, but the offer was very clear: all you had to do to get two return transatlantic flights was spend over £100 on Hoover products. Given that, at the time, a flight between London and New York cost around £200, a couple could save themselves £300 on a return trip if they bought a new Hoover. Unsurprisingly, people went out and bought Hoovers they didn't really need. Sales went through the roof. And then so did claims to redeem flights.

What Hoover hadn't realised when they extended their offer to transatlantic flights was that there had been an inevitable lag between customers buying a vacuum cleaner, washing machine or fridge, and phoning up to book seats. It was during this lag that they extended the offer to American flights, and by the time they realised that virtually everyone who had bought a Hoover product had done so because they intended to claim the flights, it was too late.

Hoover was utterly unable to deal with the enquiries. Customers spent hours waiting on the phone only to be told that the flights they wanted to book were unavailable due to demand. The offer was time limited, and pretty soon there were just no more seats available. Hoover relied on their small print to get out of offering flights to every customer, and that's when their customers took them to court.

Their customers won the case and Hoover had to pay for thousands of flights (about 220,000 people successfully claimed their free seats) at a cost of around £44 million plus legal fees. The damage to their reputation cannot be so easily measured.

Hoover made so many mistakes throughout this affair, but its biggest one was taking its customers for fools. It suggested that they were idiots for thinking that they could really get two free flights to *the USA, and when their customers challenged them, they took them to court rather than settling up. Of course £50 million is a lot of money but in the scale of Hoover's overall finances, it was a short-term write-off on their balance sheet. The cost of the decision to disrespect their customers caused long-term damage to their reputation.*

MISTAKE 27

Wrong location

IN RETAIL, I THINK WE ALL INSTINCTIVELY KNOW WHEN A shop is in the wrong place – a clothes boutique in the middle of an industrial estate is going to do less well than it would on the high street, for instance – but no matter what business you are in, if you get your location wrong you make life very hard for yourself.

When choosing where to site your business you need to find the balance between cost and convenience. In the case of a clothing boutique, it might be cheaper for it to be on an industrial estate, but it's obviously going to get fewer customers walking past its front door, which means lower revenues. It might be really convenient for the staff as they'll have ample parking, but it's very inconvenient for potential customers who do the rest of their clothes shopping on the high street. A furniture retailer on the other hand might be better suited to an out-of-town location. High-street premises are often too small to display a big enough range, and as those customers who want to collect their furniture will need convenient parking, the industrial estate makes a lot more sense. So far, so obvious, but there are other aspects of getting the right location that require more consideration.

What are the key factors?

Proximity to rivals

How close should you be to a rival? The answer varies depending on the business sector in question. If a small town had 15 shoe repair shops you would be amazed if they could all stay in business. But if there were 15 antique shops, that would be a different story, wouldn't it? There are some types of industries where competition can kill a business, and others where having a lot of similar businesses within a few minutes actually attracts additional customers. If your business is in the first category, you have to be sure that your offering is superior to the existing provider's if you intend to open up close to them. If your business is in the second category, opening up in isolation might make it very hard for you to attract customers.

Parking

I have known many small businesses go under because they underestimated the importance of parking. Adequate parking is a key component in my health clubs and I would never build a new club on a site where there was insufficient parking available. If you are unable to provide your own parking for customers and clients, then you need to look carefully at what the local authority offers. If customers can't park for free on the street outside your premises, how might their parking options affect their behaviour? I think people are more willing to pay for parking if they intend to spend an hour or more somewhere, but if they are just popping in for a few minutes to make a purchase and the chance of getting a parking ticket is pretty high, then they might reject your business and use a rival instead.

The important factor with parking is convenience. If your customers can park outside, you make yourself an easy option for them to use. If they have to park in a Pay & Display five minutes away, fiddle around for the exact change and then be anxious about getting back to their car before their ticket expires, don't be surprised if your customers exhibit signs of 'time rage'. By the time they've got to your premises they already feel like they wasted their time getting to you, and are likely to be very impatient while they're with you. Bad parking provision can actually create bad customer relations.

If you are looking for premises and you find a place that is offered significantly below the market rate, a likely reason for that is that the parking is inadequate.

Prestige

How important is it for your business to have a swanky address? Can you charge customers more just because you have an address in an upmarket part of town? I would never advise a new business to burn their money on paying extra for a prestige location although there are clearly benefits for some sorts of businesses. It's easier to attract the best staff, for instance, if you can offer them a glamorous city centre location. Transport tends to be easier in city centres, though congestion (and congestion charges) may be an issue and parking might actually be harder in the premium locations.

The right premises for the right business

Different businesses have different needs. A shoe shop, for example, needs a lot of storage room as it has to stock each shoe it sells in a range of colours and sizes. Those shoe boxes take up a lot of room and it's likely that for most shoe shops, the storage area is bigger than the shop floor. A jeweller's, by contrast, needs a large window display but relatively little storage space.

Several years ago a new arts and leisure complex – which included a gym – called ARC was built by the borough council near one of my health clubs in Stockton-on-Tees. People asked me if I was worried about the competition and I just laughed: there was no parking at ARC. The idea of gym members walking to the club, or parents taking kids to judo practice on the bus, was just silly. My only concern about ARC was as a taxpayer because it was a huge waste of public money.

Think carefully whether your business needs something specific – parking, storage or easy access to a motorway, for example – to survive. You need to work out what you want from your premises and then find somewhere that meets your specification.

Secondary locations

As a general rule, businesses that require 'footfall' – enough people walking past the door to maintain trade – benefit from being in primary locations. Businesses that are sought out by customers for a specific need, like car repairs, recruitment agencies or printers, can often do better in the cheaper secondary locations. If you need footfall, then you need to think very carefully about which premises you choose. I would suggest you stand on a busy street and count how many people walk past in an hour, then move to the cheaper secondary location and do the same. If the footfall drops off dramatically, then the chances of making a success of your business in the secondary location rapidly diminish.

I was recently waiting for my wife in a shopping centre. From my view point at the top of some escalators, I could see the entire lower floor. I focused on the flow of shoppers streaming up and down the escalators. As people went down, their eyes were naturally drawn to the shops in front of them: as soon as they stepped off the escalator they walked towards them. Only about 1 in 20 turned round at the bottom of the escalator to visit the shops behind.

Out of interest, I called the letting agent for the shopping centre and pretended I was interested in opening a shop and asked for a ballpark figure for taking a unit (yes, this is the kind of thing I do for fun!). The price differential between the units in front of and behind the escalator was approximately 25 per cent. I had to wonder if the people in the shops behind the escalator thought they had a bargain.

Online businesses

It may surprise you to know that just about everything I've just said also applies to online businesses. Should you, for instance, make yourself instantly comparable with your rivals by selling your wares through eBay or Amazon's Marketplace? Or would you be better off on your own? If you run a B&B, should you be listed on late booking engines, or stand alone?

To get the online equivalent of footfall, you have to work very hard at search engine optimisation (SEO) to make sure that your business is at the top of the results. There is no point in having a website if people don't know where to find it.

And it's also perfectly possible to have a secondary online location. If your domain name ends with a .me.uk or .ltd.uk, or if you have to go for an unusual spelling or add too many hyphens, then you make it harder for people to remember your website address. There will always be, in my opinion, a premium value for the best web suffixes – .co.uk, .net and particularly .com.

MISTAKE 28

Falling out with partners

I DON'T KNOW WHAT THE EXACT RATIO IS OF SOLO entrepreneurs to multiple person start-ups, but from my observations I reckon about half of new businesses are started by more than one person. Partnerships have advantages – a range of skills, more hands to do more work etc. – as many great businesses have proved. Innocent Drinks, Pret A Manger, Coffee Republic and The Body Shop were all founded by teams who worked well together. But partnership can also cause one huge disadvantage: aggravation.

Early on in my business career, I entered into my first and only partnership. I had been running my ice-cream business successfully for a few years and had spotted the opportunity for building and running residential care homes. It was a much bigger business than my ice-cream venture and I was a bit daunted by the responsibility. A neighbour of mine, who also ran a small local business, had also been thinking about the care home market and so we agreed to go into business together. For me, the big advantage in forming a partnership was that we could divide the workload and both continue to run our existing businesses while we launched the new one. What could possibly go wrong?

It wasn't long before the resentment started to build up. Although we owned the new company 50:50 the workload was not evenly divided. I seemed to be the only one prepared to put in the hours. I even moved into the home and slept in a sleeping bag on the floor to make sure the renovations were carried out by the flaky builders who had been hired by . . . my business partner. The same business partner who couldn't raise his share of the finance because of other complications, which of course meant that all the debt was in my name.

At times I felt utterly conned by him, at other times I was so angry I could barely look at him. I couldn't afford to buy him out of his share of the business and I couldn't risk walking away. All I could do was to carry on, make the business successful and then sell it, even if it meant my business partner would be entitled to 50 per cent of the profit. In the end, that's exactly what happened, but it was enough to put me off ever being in another partnership.

It's very difficult to value what each member of the partnership brings to the table. Do you count the hours people spend on the business? Or the money they put in? Or the profile they bring? If one person's prime role is to act as a peacemaker between the other partners, does that make their contribution as valuable as those who actually make the sales or the product? And can you put a price on a brilliant decision? Even if you could put a price on these contributions at the start of a venture, how about after six months, or six years when everyone's workload has ebbed and flowed?

There is also the delicate matter of who is actually in charge. If you can't agree on a decision, does that mean the business can't move forward? The founders of moneysupermarket.com fell out so badly that they could no longer speak to one another. One of them, Duncan Cameron, left the day-to-day running of the business and became a sleeping partner while the other, Simon Nixon, took sole charge even though Cameron held on to his stake in the business. Whatever the argument was about, it seems Nixon's ideas about strategy were right: in 2007 he bought 90 per cent of Cameron's stake for £162 million before floating the business on the Stock Exchange and raising a reported £300 million for himself.

Cameron and Nixon fell out when the business was already valuable. They both stood to lose a massive amount of money if moneysupermarket.com went under as a result of their argument, and this probably played a part in Cameron taking a back seat.

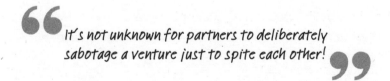

It's not unknown for partners to deliberately sabotage a venture just to spite each other!

But what happens when the founders of a business that isn't worth millions fall out and the financial penalty for failure is not so great? Very often they can bicker their way to failure. When things get really bad between founders, it's not unknown for them to deliberately sabotage a venture just to spite their partner!

It doesn't matter how much you like and respect your business partner(s) at the start of the venture, you really, truly, genuinely have no way of knowing if you will feel the same way six months, or six years, down the line. You need to take precautions at the outset. What you need, without a shadow of a doubt, is a partnership agreement.

Partnership agreement

Such an agreement sets out – in writing – what each partner's role in the venture will be. It will outline their rights and responsibilities so that each partner knows what the others expect of them. It sets out who owns what percentage of the business and who is responsible for taking key decisions.

There are no rules about what to put in a partnership agreement so you can structure the agreement, and by extension, the business any way you want to. You might agree that each partner's equity stake is conditional on their continued level of input, or conditional on the results of their input.

I would advise that there are two clauses you should absolutely always include in your partnership agreement:

Who has the final say?

If you can't agree on something, what happens? If there are more than two of you, should a democratic vote decide it? Does anyone have a veto on anyone else's decision? Ultimately, you should decide that, when push comes to shove, one of you has the duty to make a decision. Perhaps you can say that one of you has the final say about marketing while another has the final say over product development, but whatever agreement you come to, you have to agree a proper process for resolving disagreements, even if that is agreeing to abide by the toss of a coin.

What if you can't agree

You need to have a mechanism that allows you to go your separate ways with the minimum of pain. What this probably means in practicality is that a buy-out mechanism needs to be agreed in advance. One way to do this is to agree that any partner can buy out the other for a percentage, or multiple, of profit. Another way is for each partner to offer sealed bids for the company to the other. Whoever is prepared to pay the higher amount should be allowed to buy the other partner's stake.

Other things you might want to include in your partnership agreement are dispute resolution, a cooling-off period or a differential split between equity and income depending on the contribution each person makes.

Starting a business is always harder than you think, and can put undue strain on working relationships. Tempers always flare. Opinions always differ. Most people can accept this and work through minor irritations, but if those irritations become more serious, it will really help if you all understand your responsibilities to the business, and to each other.

MISTAKE 29

Outrageous valuations

Q: What's a sure-fire way to annoy a Dragon?
A: By ridiculously overvaluing your business.

One of the few rules of *Dragons' Den* is that entrepreneurs must say how much investment they are looking for because they are only allowed to leave the Den with at least the stated amount, or nothing at all. What this means is that the majority of opening statements end with the entrepreneur saying 'and we are looking for £x in exchange for y per cent of the business'. This instantly enables the Dragons, and viewers, to know how much the entrepreneurs value their business at. I would say that more than 90 per cent of visitors to the Den overvalue their business. Sometimes that's just to build in some negotiation room, but more often than not it's because they have no idea how to value their business.

When an entrepreneur says they are looking for £100,000 investment in exchange for 10 per cent of their business, my first question is: what makes your business worth a million quid? The sorts of answers I usually get include:

1   This business is such a great opportunity in such a brilliant market, that it's worth it.

2   In two years' time, our income will be zillions, therefore this represents a sober valuation.

3   We've put £100,000 of our own money in, and our time and effort represents several times that amount.

Any variation on these answers can usually guarantee that I will shortly declare myself out. If an entrepreneur is that clueless about valuation – and that arrogant – then the chances that they will one day end up running a multimillion-pound venture are very close to zero.

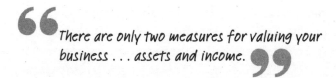

There are only two measures for valuing your business . . . assets and income.

Entrepreneurs often inflate the value of their time and effort, the brilliance of their idea or the size of the opportunity, but the fact is there are really only two things that count towards a sound valuation of a business – assets and income. And if you have any debt, then that needs to be deducted from your valuation. So that means if your business hasn't yet produced an income and does not own any assets, then your business has a valuation of . . . zero.

How to accurately value your business

As a rule of thumb, I think a fair valuation for a new business is three times next year's profits. So if you think your business will produce profits of £80,000 next year – and that's *profit*, not turnover – then I would value your business at £240,000. If you had assets – usually stock or premises – then I would add that to the valuation, and deduct any debt.

For established businesses, it is actually quite straightforward to value your business as there are standard multiples used for most industries. This figure is either based on previous sales of businesses in your sector, or on the valuation of publicly listed companies in your sector. You can find this figure in the *Financial Times* where businesses' incomes and valuations are listed. To get the multiple for your industry, find a listing for a business in your sector and divide its valuation by its income. In the health club industry, the multiple is around 9 for freehold clubs, and 3 for leasehold clubs (although it used to be higher before the recession, around 6 times profit). So if a health club business comes up for sale, I can quickly work out how much I would be prepared to pay for it.

Getting your valuation wrong might not be the worst thing an ambitious and tenacious entrepreneur can do, but if you need investment or a loan, you won't have many opportunities to get the money you need. If you blow your chance when it comes along, you might not get another go at putting things right.

Perhaps more important than that is that if you kid yourself you're running a multimillion-pound business when you're not, you might make decisions that are inappropriate for your business.

And let's not forget, no one likes someone who's too big for their boots.

MISTAKE 30

MANY PEOPLE STILL BELIEVE THAT GETTING A PATENT CAN protect your business from rivals. This is a myth. In the vast majority of cases, patents are a) expensive, b) time consuming and c) pointless.

Let me give you the example of the very first business to be shown in the first series of *Dragons' Den*. It was an invention called the Baby Dream Machine, a device you put under the wheels of a pram to rock a baby to sleep. Any parent who has ever tried to put a crying baby down knows how valuable an invention this could be, which is why I made the owners an offer of investment but their valuation of the business was so high, they had the cheek to reject it! Undaunted, the Baby Dream Machine owners came back into the Den in the second series hoping that, having sorted out our concerns about their valuation, we would reconsider investing. We might well have done, were it not for the fact that in the intervening year another pram-rocking device had come on the market. Having a patent couldn't, and didn't, defend the Baby Dream Machine from a rival product launching.

> *Patents don't protect ideas, they only protect unique technological innovation.*

That's because patents don't protect ideas, they only protect unique technological innovation. The Baby Dream Machine may have had patented components, but the *idea* of a machine that rocks a pram is beyond the scope of patent law, so as long as the rival used a different mechanism to make the pram move, there was no infringement of the Baby Dream Machine's patent.

To patent or not to patent

It's been my experience in the Den that patents are of quite limited use for new businesses, so I'd just like to run through the reasons why you should think very carefully before spending time and money trying to get a patent on your product.

1   It's entirely possible that *the patent you seek may not be granted*. Just because you don't know about a similar product or technology, it doesn't mean that it doesn't

exist. Someone may have already registered a patent for something so similar to your invention that your patent won't be granted. Of course, you won't know this until you have spent time and money on the application process.

2   *Getting a patent can be expensive.* This is especially so if you use a patent lawyer to write the patent for you, which is something I'd recommend as your patent needs to be precise if it's going to a) be granted, and b) be useful. You're probably looking at £5–10k in fees – though you can fill in the necessary forms yourself free of charge – and you have to ask yourself if that money might not be better spent on something else, and if it will give you a genuine commercial advantage that's worth more than you spent getting the patent in the first place.

3   Even if your patent is granted, the only way to prove that a rival has infringed your patent is by embarking on a long and costly legal case. Keep in mind that *there are no patent police.* If someone infringes your patent, no one will knock on their door and take them in for questioning. It will be down to you to a) spot the offence, and b) prosecute the offence. Such legal action would be expensive, so you have to be realistic about whether you would actually bother to enforce your patent in such a situation, especially if the company infringing your patent is a huge multinational with its own in-house legal team.

4 *The patent process usually takes years.* It might be a really unnecessary distraction for you as you try to get your business off the ground.

5 *Patents only apply in the country in which they are filed.* If you want global protection, you have to apply for patents in every territory, taking up more time you don't have, and more money you could be spending on something else.

Other ways to protect your idea

One of the most successful inventions to have come into the Den has been the Kymera Magic Wand Remote Control, a truly magical product that you can use instead of boring old remote controls for your TV, hi-fi or – if you're particularly flash – your lighting. Anything that has previously been controlled by pushing buttons on a grey rectangle of plastic can now be conjured into life with a wizardly wand. No wonder all five Dragons wanted to invest.

The wand was developed by Chris Barnardo and Richard Blakesley, two people with enough experience of the technology sector to understand the value of patents. They knew that they couldn't stop someone else from launching a wand-shaped remote control, so they looked into other ways to protect their idea and their business.

1 They realised it was *vital not to talk about their invention to anyone outside the business*. This might seem insignificant, but if you work in an industry where your friends and colleagues have the occasional drink with someone from a rival company, it's amazing how quickly a piece of gossip or information can travel. As soon as something is deemed to be in the public domain, you cannot get a patent on it.

2 When they did talk to people – they had to discuss their invention with the company that would manufacture the wand, and the companies that would sell it – they did so with *the protection of non-disclosure agreements* (NDAs) that prevent the people who sign them discussing your negotiations with anyone else. An NDA provides a decent level of protection for an idea pre-launch, but once something is in the public domain anyone – including those who have signed NDAs – can copy your idea.

3 They filed for *design and trademark registrations*, both of which are easier, cheaper and quicker than obtaining patent registrations and offer a good level of protection if someone copies your idea too closely, or tries to pass off their product as yours.

4 They signed *watertight contracts that guaranteed exclusivity*. The manufacturer was prevented from making any other kind of wand, and their distributors were prevented from selling any rival product.

5 They built *fantastic relationships with retailers*, offering them great service and reliability, thereby reducing the likelihood that those retailers would want to get their wands from anyone else.

6 They made *the best product* they possibly could so that they were confident any competitor product would be inferior and therefore provide less of a threat.

Their wand is also now protected by several patents, but what was so smart about the way Chris and Richard went about getting their patents is that they didn't spend their start-up capital obtaining them. Instead they waited until the cost could be justified by the return. They initially filed for the patent themselves – remember, their background is in technology businesses so they weren't complete novices – but when the business started to produce revenues, they hired a patent attorney to make sure everything was watertight. By this time, the technology in the wand had developed, and so the patent they finally obtained was more comprehensive than the one originally applied for.

The patents on the Kymera don't just offer protection to Chris and Richard, they also offer protection to investors, which reduces the risk for someone taking a stake in the business, which was undoubtedly a factor in all five Dragons making them an offer. If you think your business will seek investment at some point, then there is an added reason to seek a patent.

However, if you have sought a patent in the misguided belief that it is a badge of honour, or an endorsement of your idea and your product, then an investor will question your priorities and your judgement. Entrepreneurs should think long and hard before embarking on patent registration, but not too long or too hard: the chances are there is something much more important you should be doing with your time and your money.

The Intellectual Property Office's website (www.ipo.gov. uk) is the place to seek further advice and the necessary forms.

MISTAKE 31

Arrogance

I LIKE TO THINK THAT I KNOW QUITE A LOT ABOUT business. Over more than 30 years, I have made money in a wide range of sectors from selling ice creams to residential care for the elderly, to property, health clubs, children's day care and hotels. I've also sat on the board of, or invested in, businesses in other sectors including a radio station, refrigerated transport, children's stage schools, electronics manufacturers and a cleaning company. But just because I've learned something about those businesses and those sectors, it doesn't mean I know everything about every business. Yet I see an awful of lot of experienced business people come unstuck because they think they can transfer their skills and knowledge from one business to the next. Some skills, like preparing accounts or selling, are universal, but some are so sector-specific that you won't know about them until you experience them first-hand.

Knowing your onions

One of the reasons I have thoroughly enjoyed working on *Dragons' Den* is because I have learned so much. Sitting next to Theo Paphitis, in particular, for the past six years has been a real education because he knows pretty much everything there is to know about retail.

Before I'd sat next to Theo, I'd never given an awful lot of thought to how much packaging a product comes with, and if I had, I would have thought about design or the environmental impact of the packaging. Theo thinks about volume. More precisely, he thinks, 'How many of those can I fit on a shelf?' Something in a big-box takes up a lot of shelf space, and as shelf space is prime real estate to a retailer, he's looking at big-box items to also be big-ticket items. I've noticed he's very fond of products that can be displayed on hooks, because hook space is much cheaper to a retailer than shelf space. Although this makes perfect sense, it's the kind of detail you just wouldn't know about unless you'd been in retail yourself.

One of the *Dragons' Den* presentations I learned the most from was by a shoe designer. I wasn't particularly interested in getting into the shoe business – I prefer show business! – and as soon as I heard Theo's assessment of the opportunity it confirmed my hunch that it wasn't an industry for me. In fashion, you have to have every product in every size and a range of colours. In the case of the underwear Theo sells in his Boux Avenue stores, this doesn't take up a lot of storage space, but shoes? Those boxes have got to go somewhere. And as the unit price of a pair of handmade leather shoes is considerably higher than the price of a pair of Theo's knickers, the cost of acquiring the stock is enormous. And we haven't even got round to the waste. If your designs aren't popular, you can discount them by 50 per cent, maybe even 70 per cent, and still not sell them. And let's not forget that shoe retailers have to stock the tiny sizes and the giant sizes even though the chances are they will have difficulty selling them. The more I listened, the more I realised the less I knew.

Over the years I have met many entrepreneurs who think they can make a going concern of any business in any sector because they are 'in the business of business'. And of course, because they're confident about their business skills, they often jump into new businesses with two feet . . . and an open wallet.

Another Dragon, James Caan, was very open in his autobiography about his failure to turn around the sandwich chain Benjy's. The business was put up for sale by administrators and James thought his experience of business would be enough to turn the venture round. He walked into several branches of Benjy's and thought it was pretty obvious why the once-successful chain had gone into administration: in the early days, Benjy's had thrived on selling cheap and traditional sandwiches and soups to the mass market; it had lost its way trying to compete with the likes of Pret A Manger by selling wraps and fancy salads. All Benjy's needed to do was go back to basics. Having identified the problem, James took on the running of Benjy's, optimistic that he could turn it around. After all, how hard can it be to make a sandwich?

Of course, things turned out to be a lot more complicated than James had imagined. The machinery in the kitchens was designed to make certain sorts of sandwiches and in some cases a change in menu meant retooling the equipment. It also turned out that the business had contracts to buy certain ingredients which meant James had a choice: either they bought the ingredients they no longer wanted, or they bought their way out of the contracts. And James's plan to shut down the poorest-performing branches hit a snag when he discovered he couldn't terminate the leases without paying a penalty.

James clearly knows a lot about business, but he didn't know enough about the *sandwich* business.

In 2009, James told me that he was making a substantial investment in a chain of health clubs. 'I don't think we'll be in competition with your clubs,' he said. 'We're going for a different market.' James told me his clubs would be the EasyJet of gyms offering a low-cost, no-frills service. By not offering a swimming pool and by not including the cost of fitness classes in the membership fee, James's Nuyuu gyms would charge £19.99 a month to members, which is around half of what Bannatyne members pay. Do you think I was worried? Not a bit.

Why? Because I know the health club market as well as anyone else in the country and I know what will make people join a gym. The steam and sauna rooms are just as important as the treadmills and leg presses. And the pool is an absolute necessity. What Bannatyne's offers is affordable luxury; what Nuyuu was offering might have been affordable, but it would only appeal to a very small market. Even when Nuyuu opened in Livingston where I have a club, I wasn't worried it would take members away.

James encountered all the problems with recruiting members that I thought he would, and he also encountered another problem: the kind of people who want to pay £19.99 a month are also sometimes the kind of people that will either try and get away without paying, or will struggle to pay. Nuyuu had a lot of problems with cancelled direct debits. The Livingston branch was shut down, and other branches were sold 'for an undisclosed sum' to the Energie chain. 'An undisclosed sum', in my experience, is a euphemism for a loss.

James isn't the only experienced entrepreneur who's come a cropper when taking his talent and knowledge from one sector to another: Virgin Brides, anyone? It's almost always the case that the more successful you've been, the easier it is to fail the next time.

To make sure it never happens to you, you need to think like a mountaineer. I'm serious! Mountaineers always talk about respecting the mountain. Blizzards, avalanches, crevasses, frozen equipment or any number of other perils can bring a quick end to the expeditions of the most experienced climbers. It's the same in business: if you don't show business enough respect, you tend to get punished.

Case study 5: Woolworths

Woolworths was a much-loved fixture on the British high street throughout the 20th century. Its first store opened in Liverpool in 1909, and 99 years later, in January 2008, nearly a thousand branches closed their doors for the last time.

Woolworths was a shop we all knew. Loads of us bought our first records in a branch of Woolies, or spent our pocket money in there on Pick'n'mix or toys. As adults, Woolworths became a reliable source for things no one else on the high street seemed to stock any more – like sewing thread, school uniforms and fuses. There weren't many people in Britain who had never shopped in Woolies. And yet now it is no more. So what happened?

The seeds of failure were probably sown in 2001 when Woolworths' parent company Kingfisher plc demerged Woolies to become a stand-alone business. At the time of the demerger, Woolworths was saddled with a lot of the parent company's debt, which meant the pressure was on for the newly independent Woolies to make sufficient profit to meet its repayments. Presumably the new bosses did a sensitivity analysis, but they can't have really looked at the findings very closely. If they had, Woolworths might still be around. Sales in virtually every department started to slide as out-of-town supermarkets started selling crockery, cookware, stationery and kids' clothes that had once been a core part of Woolworths' business. Simultaneously, high-street sales of music nosedived as fans bought MP3s online. Only Woolies' Pick'n'mix maintained its market share. But at £1.99 a bag, you've got to sell a lot of sweets to make ends meet.

The instore mix of cookware, sweets, toys and DIY essentials was as confused as the structure of the business as a whole. As well as its high-street stores, Woolworths simultaneously attempted to be a catalogue retailer to rival Tesco and Argos with its Big Red Book. And it also moved into out-of-town retail parks with its giant Big W stores. In addition, it was also trying to be an online retailer and capitalise on the fact that it owned a book and music distribution business. It was just too complicated.

By the middle of 2008, it was clear that Woolworths was a business in a lot of trouble, but its problems shouldn't have been enough to bring its days to an end. In better financial times, they wouldn't have been. Someone would have bought the retailer, or the board would have hired a CEO with the passion to turn things around, and Woolworths would have been well-placed as Britain recovered from the recession.

In the end, Woolworths was a victim of the credit crunch. It couldn't restructure its loans after the banks tightened their lending criteria, so it had no choice but to default on those loans, which in turn meant the financial authorities had no choice but to appoint administrators for the business. Woolies was gone.

So Woolies' biggest mistake was thinking that the market would never change – both the retail market and the money-lending market. Although it must have known about the threats from supermarkets and online retailers, Woolworths did not react quickly or strongly enough. It thought its brand and track record would mean it could always borrow money when it needed to. The sad fact is that Woolworths didn't change with the world around it.

MISTAKE 32

Whose money is it anyway?

IT DOESN'T MATTER IF THEY'RE RUNNING A CORNER SHOP or an international conglomerate, there are some CEOs that keep confusing their company's money with their own. Usually this is down to incompetence, but occasionally it's downright fraudulent.

It's understandable that an owner of a business who has put their own money into a venture is quite likely to feel entitled to take money out of it. And whether they take the money out of the till before shutting up shop on a Friday night or as a director's loan, it's all the owner's money anyway so it doesn't matter, right?

I'm not surprised that many CEOs and company founders don't take a regular salary. The UK's tax laws encourage business owners to pay themselves in dividends (i.e., as a share of the profit) so they don't have to pay employers' National

Insurance contributions on their salary, thus reducing the cost to the business. Although the muddling of the company's and individual's money is understandable, it doesn't make it good for business, so I'd like to run through some of the mistakes I've come across.

Taking money out of the till

Let's take the example of a typical corner shop where the owner takes £20 out to give their child some pocket money, or £150 out to pay for a wholesale delivery. At the end of the month, or the year, the owner still has the same amount of money they would have had, the child gets its pocket money and the supplier gets paid.

The problem with that is that the pocket money reduces the turnover, which reduces the profit, which reduces the tax, which is technically . . . illegal. And while the supplier might like getting paid in cash, if a proper record of the payment isn't made the owner might wonder why their turnover suddenly plummeted one day.

But the big reason why this is no way to run a business is that you have no accurate record of your costs, your turnover or your profits. Which means you have no figures to analyse to see where you are overspending, or under-earning, or how you can increase your margins.

Of course, you don't have to physically take actual notes out of an actual till to be guilty of this. Any time you transfer untaxed money out of the company and into another account – by cheque, by transfer, by paying for something which is not for the company's benefit – you lose your ability to accurately assess your business.

Mistaking profit for salary

I lost count a long time ago of people who told me their business produces profits of, let's say, £100k a year. I would then ask them what salary they were on, and they would then say they took the £100k as their income. Which of course means that their business doesn't make any profit.

When people sell small- and medium-sized businesses – the kind you see in the 'Businesses for sale' listings in local papers – they are usually sold on the basis of the profit they make. Every week I see shops and franchises promising profits of £30k a year, or so, when they mean it has the potential to produce an income for the owner of £30k a year. It amazes me how people don't realise that their profit is the sum left in the business, not the sum left in their personal bank account.

Director's loans

If you put £100 into a company as equity you cannot take it out without selling shares, taking it as a dividend or as wages, all of which are taxable. However, if you put the money in as a loan to the company you are entitled to take that £100 out at any point. If you take £120 out, then the extra £20 is now treated as a loan from the company to you, and this is called a Director's Loan. And like any other loan, it needs to be repaid. So long as the money is returned within the same accounting period then you don't have to inform HM Revenue & Customs. But if the loan is unpaid, then the amount becomes taxable. This makes it a very expensive loan – tax rates are significantly higher than interest rates – and can completely mess up your cashflow. However, if the loan is subsequently repaid to the company, that tax can be reclaimed so long as repayment is made within six years.

> **Taking short-term gains can have a detrimental impact on your long-term profits.**

In the early days of a business it can be very difficult to know what to pay yourself, but my advice would be to pay yourself as little as possible for as long as possible until you have a clear idea of revenues throughout the year. If there is something left over at the end of the year, you can either leave it in the business, or take a portion of it as a bonus. Once you understand the kinds of revenues your company is capable of producing, you can increase your regular payments.

If the business has a spike in profits, that might be an opportunity to invest in expansion rather than giving yourself a pay rise. Taking short-term gains can have a detrimental impact on your long-term profits.

However you decide to take your income, it is important that you keep detailed records of all transactions. If you ever want a loan or investment, then you will have your accounts scrutinised. And if HM Revenue & Customs wants to take a look at your books, you better hope you made a note of the £20 you handed out in pocket money.

MISTAKE 33

Growing too quickly

TO PARAPHRASE MICHAEL DOUGLAS'S CHARACTER GORDON Gekko in *Wall Street*, growth is good. Rapid growth, on the other hand, is extremely risky.

When I started my care home business in the 1980s, I was impatient to expand as quickly as possible. I knew that every time I built a new home and filled it with residents, my profits would leap up. So as soon as one home was built and occupied, I remortgaged it to release capital and built another. If the right plots of land came up, I would try and build two homes simultaneously.

The builders constantly needed paying and at times I just couldn't raise any more capital. At one point I had two half-built homes, which represented a massive amount of capital I had taken out of the business and that I had no chance of getting any income from. Eventually I managed to rearrange finance and resume construction, but there were many times in the early years where my impatience put a strain on the business.

The 1980s was a time of relatively easy lending. If the credit crunch of 2008 had happened 20 years previously, I don't know if those care homes would still be unfinished. And if I hadn't fixed my interest rates in the early 1980s, the 15 per cent rates we had at the end of the decade might also have finished my business off. I didn't really appreciate it at the time, but my rapid rate of growth left my new business vulnerable to changes in the lending climate. I got away with it, but many businesses in the 2008 credit crunch didn't.

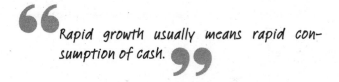

Rapid growth usually means rapid consumption of cash.

Rapid growth usually means a rapid consumption of money, and when you are spending money quickly, you can't be sure you're spending it wisely. What if you buy too much of the wrong stock or hire too many members of staff who aren't up to the job? Or what happens if your company is caught completely unawares by the public's response to an advertising campaign and unable to fulfil orders, answer enquiries and generally satisfy demand?

Red Letter Days

Generally, rapid expansion is a mistake made by new companies, but that's not always the case. Rachel Elnaugh, who was on the panel for the first two series of *Dragons' Den*, had been running her events company Red Letter Days for over a decade before she ran into trouble. Red Letter Days sold 'experience' gift vouchers for things like hot-air balloon flights and driving days at Brands Hatch. Customers paid upfront for the voucher, which meant Red Letter Days had very positive cashflow as it would often be months before the voucher was redeemed. The company made a small profit on every voucher, but made its real money when recipients of the vouchers failed to cash them in.

Rachel decided to push Red Letter Days with a very expensive TV advertising campaign. In anticipation of a good response, she had hired new people and had a massive team, according to press reports, of 130 employees. Some of them had very senior positions as this coincided with Rachel taking a back seat to have her fourth child.

Obviously the staff increases and advertising costs were incurred before any increase in revenue from the big push, so that had an impact on the company's normally buoyant cashflow. But the campaign had an unintended consequence – it reminded thousands of people of the vouchers they had at the bottom of their drawer and led to an unusually high level of people cashing them in, which again hit cashflow. And when the advertising campaign failed to pull in enough new customers, the cracks started to appear.

Red Letter Days was then dealt another blow: the credit card companies which processed the majority of customer payments changed their terms and conditions. Because anyone making a purchase via a credit card automatically gets their purchase insured. The card companies started holding on to a small percentage of the funds to cover the insurance. Red Letter Days' margins weren't big enough to cope and the company went into administration.

The best way to scale up

Even if your business isn't caught out by external factors during a period of rapid expansion, there are other dangers in expanding too quickly that can harm the efficiency of your business. For instance, if you're looking to increase your workforce, you can't just put more people in an office and expect them to know what to do. Who hires them, manages them and is on hand to make them feel like part of a team? Businesses that grow at a more organic pace tend to have more cohesive teams who understand and promote the company's values.

Rapid expansion can prevent the people leading the business from assessing their progress with accuracy. There's simply no time to sit down and ask themselves: 'What are we getting right?' and 'Where are we missing a trick?' Without that time for reflection, important lessons aren't learned.

You can think of a rapidly expanding company being built like a tower of Jenga bricks. You can build a tall tower as quickly as bricks become available, but the taller it becomes the more unstable it will be and the more prone it will be to collapse. One small change to your credit card provider's terms and conditions could be all it takes. That's because your tower has scale without structure, and that structure is as important to a business as steel girders are to skyscrapers.

One of the reasons behind the success of Bannatyne Fitness has been the inherent strength of our internal structures. We have been able to expand successfully because we have a regional reporting structure that decentralises a lot of the day-to-day decision making. Our teams report to club managers who report to regional managers who report to the Managing Director.

Putting efficient and robust structures in place takes time, and that has the effect of naturally slowing the pace of expansion to sensible levels. I completely understand an entrepreneur's impatience to grow as quickly as possible – I have been impatient myself – but if you take the time to get your structure right, you can slowly scale up your business more reliably and more successfully.

Case study 6: Barings Bank

Most people remember the story of Nick Leeson and how the 'rogue trader' brought down one of the world's oldest merchant banks. And most people think Leeson is the reason why the bank went bust. They're only partially right.

In 1992, Nick Leeson started working for Barings Bank in Singapore as their Head of Settlements. He also traded futures on SIMEX, the Singapore International Monetary Exchange, and it seems he was pretty good at it: his trades accounted for 10 per cent of Barings worldwide earnings of £100 million. No wonder, then, that his bosses were quite happy to let Leeson do whatever he thought needed to be done. He was their star, and they saw their job was simply to let him shine.

Leeson was promoted to Head of Trading and it seems his confidence increased and he placed bigger and bigger trades. Dealing in futures is a particularly risky and volatile form of trading that predicts the future levels of stock markets. Leeson was effectively betting on whether he thought the Japanese Nikkei index would climb or fall. Normally futures traders 'hedge' their positions so that they make a profit no matter which way the market goes, but Leeson – presumably brimming with confidence after years of successful trading – decided to maximise his profits by not hedging, i.e., if he thought the market would go up, he wouldn't hedge for a fall. If he was right, fantastic; if he was wrong, disaster.

Had Leeson just made a few bad trades and lost a lot of money, he wouldn't have ended up in jail. He compounded his losses by fraudulently hiding them from his bosses in a phantom account, and he could do this because when his bosses had made him Head of Trading, they hadn't stripped him of his title of Head of Settlements. Leeson was perfectly placed to cover up his mistakes, but only in the short term. Eventually he knew someone would come looking for the lost money. So all he had to do was place some trades that made money and recoup the losses.

Only, of course, he didn't make any money. In fact he continued to lose it at a spectacular rate and his only hope of recovering the accumulated losses was to make bigger and bigger bets in the hope his luck, or his judgement, changed. It didn't. Knowing he was about to be found out, Leeson went on the run as the bank's bosses tried to put a rescue package together with the help of the Bank of England. Such a deal proved impossible and Barings was declared insolvent in February 1995 owing $1.4 billion.

Obviously, the person who takes most of the blame for the fate of Barings is Leeson himself, and he was rightly jailed for his fraud. However, the way I see it, his bosses weren't entirely without blame. They had made one of the biggest mistakes in business: they didn't know how to manage their staff.

Looking back it seems unbelievable that Leeson was allowed to keep his job as Head of Settlements. That should never have happened. It also seems implausible that no one questioned why a previously stellar performer was not producing the millions of dollars of profits he had done the year before. No one was adequately auditing Leeson's performance, and no one was actually managing him. He was a young man earning a vast salary while living a long way from home and yet none of his bosses thought about paying him a visit, taking him to one side and saying, 'How's it going, Nick, fancy a drink tonight?'

Leeson's actions were illegal, but his bosses' lack of action is a textbook case of bad management. If you think that bad management can't make that much difference to your bottom line, just remember Barings.

MISTAKE

34

THERE IS A LIMIT TO HOW MUCH ONE PERSON CAN ACHIEVE on their own. Even a really, truly brilliant entrepreneur can only work so many hours a day for so long. No one has every skill needed to make a success of a business. And that means that if you want to be successful in business, you have to be good at delegating. So here are my rules on how to delegate.

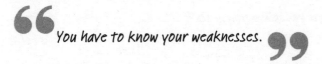

You have to know your weaknesses.

What to delegate?

The most important question to ask yourself is this: what can be done better by someone else? To answer the question you have to know your weaknesses. We all have some bits of our job we enjoy more than others, and looking at the tasks you don't enjoy isn't the dumbest place to start looking for jobs to give to someone else. However, if you don't enjoy a job, the chances are someone else won't enjoy it either, and without the motivation to make a success of their own business, an employee is likely to do those tasks less well than you.

Ideally you're looking to delegate tasks that:

- Someone else is better at than you (sales, accountancy, menial tasks)
- Someone else can do more quickly than you (this boosts your productivity)
- Free you up to think strategically and allow you to grow your business
- Are cheaper done by someone other than you

This might well mean giving up the parts of your job that you enjoy the most, but if it means you can grow your business, then that's a sacrifice worth making.

Who to delegate to?

Once you've decided what to delegate, you need to find the right person to delegate those tasks to. The key here is that the person should fit the position. There's no point deciding that you are going to delegate your accountancy and then hand the task over to someone who's never used a spreadsheet. Equally there's no point giving a very able and ambitious person tedious and menial tasks as they will quickly become demoralised and disruptive.

New businesses sometimes have the opposite problem: instead of hiring the right kind of person for the right kind of role, a small team of founders have to divide up the tasks between them. This might be easy if one person is a technical genius, another is brilliant at sales and a third is a strategic thinker, but the chances are that each individual's skills won't perfectly fit the available roles. In this situation, you have to put the team first and the individuals second: some people might not be deployed to make the best of their ability while others will take on tasks they'd rather not have to do, but when it's your company you ultimately share in the success of the team as a whole.

If you don't have enough work to give to an employee, then you should look into delegating key tasks to third parties. If you get an accountant to do your books, you are actually delegating that job. Or if you get a call centre to filter your calls, you are also delegating. You don't have to employ someone to delegate to them.

Whether you're part of a team of founders or you are hiring new staff from scratch, the ideal people to work with are those whose skills complement yours.

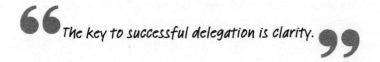

The key to successful delegation is clarity.

How to delegate

The key to successful delegation is clarity. Be clear about what you want doing, how you want it doing and by when. It really is that simple.

1 Explain – clearly – what you want done.

2 Give someone the tools they need to get the job done.

3 Convey the principles and values you want them to adhere to.

4 If appropriate, give someone a budget to work within.

5 Give them a deadline for the work.

6 Let them know how their work will be assessed and what impact it will have on the rest of the business.

7 Let them know they can come to you if they have a problem.

8 *Then let them get on with it.*

Letting someone get on with a task that you used to do yourself is something I know a lot of new entrepreneurs struggle with. The temptation to suggest better ways of doing it, or checking to see if they are doing it the same way you did it, or even just being very curious to know how they're finding things are all behaviours that can scupper effective delegation. If you micromanage people you stifle and frustrate them and you rob them of the chance to learn things for themselves.

So long as you have been through points 1 to 7 above with them, it doesn't matter how they spend each minute of their day, or what their interim successes are. All that matters is that they know what is expected of them, and so long as they meet the deadline you have given them, you shouldn't be bothered with the minutiae. The whole point of delegation is that it frees up your time so you can achieve more. The entire process is pointless if you then spend your time worrying about what your team is up to and finding subtle and not-so-subtle ways to check up on them. The only way you're going to find out if they are up to the job is if you let them get on with it.

You have been told!

MISTAKE

35

Not knowing your KPI from your elbow

It's not just about profit

How do you know if your business is doing well? Do you look at your profit? Or the level of sales? Or the number of customers? The answer will vary from company to company and from industry to industry, and it's harder to know what measure to use the bigger your business is and the longer it's been in operation. All of which makes it vital to identify your Key Performance Indicators (KPIs).

The easiest way to measure how a business is performing is to look at its profit and see whether it is making more this year than it did last year. But believe it or not, an increase in profit isn't necessarily a good thing. Honestly. If that increase has come at the expense of quality or service or reputation, then it is likely that holding on to existing customers and acquiring new ones will become harder, which means next year's profits might suffer.

There are all sorts of reasons why profit isn't always the most helpful figure to focus on. In a year of exceptional costs – for example, when you had half your workforce on parental leave – your profit won't necessarily reflect the strength of the business. Or if the economy worsened, a dip in profits might actually be a mark of success if your rivals' profits slumped further than yours.

Profit alone is a blunt tool for measuring a business.

Don't get me wrong, profit is ultimately the most important measurement of success – if you don't have any, then you will go out of business – but on its own it's a very blunt tool. If you think about your friends and family for a moment, you don't just judge how well they're doing on the basis of their salary, do you? You might consider whether they have a good work/ life balance, or look at their health, the holidays they take or the social life they have. Money helps, of course, but your richest friend won't necessarily be your happiest.

As businesses mature, the rate at which they grow changes. Often, the early years of rapid expansion are replaced with sober years of consolidation. So measuring growth isn't always an indication of progress either. If profits are hampered by the economy and growth is sluggish, does this automatically mean your business is in trouble? You wouldn't know unless you had identified the KPIs that keep you focused on what matters. KPIs are absolutely vital to established businesses as they give you relevant benchmarks to compare yourself against.

Measures that matter

So what kinds of things should you be measuring? The answer will be specific to your company, but there are a couple of things to consider that will help you decide what KPIs would best help your business.

Relevance

Your KPIs should be aimed at monitoring your core business activities. So if you were to operate a mail order business, for example, you might think a good way of assessing how well you were doing is the percentage of deliveries that were received on time. If you manufacture a product, you might find knowing how many hours it takes to produce 100 of them would be really useful information.

You can also use KPIs to monitor progress within different departments of your business. You might, for instance, ask your head of finance to monitor what proportion of your invoices are paid on time. Or ask your sales managers what the call-to-sale ratio is, or what percentage of sales come from existing customers.

KPIs change as your business evolves. For instance, if you had recently opened a hotel, your occupancy rate would be a very relevant KPI. Once your hotel has been open for a few years and your occupancy rate can't be substantially increased, then monitoring your income per guest might be a better way to gauge your business's performance.

Measurable

For KPIs to be useful they have to be measurable, and consistently measurable. For instance, it is very difficult to measure the happiness of your staff, but you can measure your staff turnover rate, which would give you a good idea of the job satisfaction of your staff. You can't measure how satisfied your customers are – even if you survey them, the information is still subjective – but you can record how many come back for a repeat purchase and how often.

Data

KPIs are brilliant at turning hunches into data. You might suspect that your sales team aren't getting results quickly enough. A drop in the call-to-sale ratio would prove it. If you think your manufacturing costs are too high, the right KPI will help you assess the level of wastage in your processes. And once you have that data you can make decisions. For instance, you can calculate how much to spend on sales training to improve the call-to-sale ratio and at what point the training pays for itself. There's no point in having KPIs if you don't make changes once you have the data in front of you.

KPIs are particularly useful to me in my businesses. Bannatyne Fitness is now a well-established business and it's unlikely we'll grow rapidly (except through a timely acquisition, which is something you can never rule out) in the immediate future. We made the decision to absorb the VAT rise in 2011 (from 17.5 to 20 per cent) so this will impact on our profits. How then can I tell if my team are doing well? By using KPIs.

I delegate the day-to-day running of Bannatyne Fitness to my Chief Executive Nigel Armstrong, and I measure his success by using a range of KPIs. Staff turnover is one of our KPIs, as a low turnover saves on recruitment and training costs; another is our profit-per-member, which focuses Nigel's attention on keeping a lid on costs and finding new ways – like offering spa and beauty treatments – to get our members to spend more time and, of course, money with us.

In previous years, our KPIs have been different. At one point it was our churn rate – i.e., the percentage of our members who did not renew their membership – as I instinctively knew it was too high. Once we reduced our churn rate, a different KPI was needed. Profit-per-member is currently the best indicator I use to assess the health of the business, but ask me in a few years' time and it will probably have changed again.

MISTAKE 36

Failing to manage staff

THE SINGLE BIGGEST EXPENSE MOST COMPANIES INCUR is the wage bill. The most valuable asset of any company walks out of the door each night. Get your staffing wrong, and you may as well just shut up shop.

> *When your staff start managing you, it is a disaster.*

I have known business people who are scared of their staff. They don't like the way their team does something, or the way clients are spoken to, yet they feel incapable of saying anything. They don't want to upset people or be seen as a bully, or they are worried that a confrontation will lead to a resignation. Needless to say, when your staff start managing you it is a recipe for business disaster.

I've also known managers who want so much to be liked that they award undeserved bonuses or spend far too much on team-building away days or, more damagingly, give people positions that they are not qualified for. And then, of course, there are those who resent their staff and see them as a drain on the company's resources.

So how do you get it right? By always remembering that you don't have 'staff', you have 'a team'. And just as in sport, teams need to work together, to complement each other and to understand shared short- and long-term goals. I've already gone through the importance of delegation, but there are other aspects of managing a team that can make a significant difference to the productivity and happiness of your workforce.

Pay and conditions

As paying salaries is likely to be your biggest expense, it makes sense to try and keep your wage bill as low as possible. But if you are too mean with your wages, you are going to have a miserable workforce and – more than likely – a disruptive and costly level of staff turnover. You can get a good idea of what the going rate for a particular position is by looking at recruitment advertising (which is more likely to be online than in the papers these days) placed by rival companies hiring for similar positions.

A good local recruitment consultant should be able to advise you (for a fee, of course), or if you have industry contacts you could ask around for an acceptable ballpark figure.

In Britain, we rarely talk about what we earn, but if one of your employees suspects they are being paid less than a colleague doing the same job, then resentment is going to build up. It can be very helpful for organisations to have pay bands for various positions, so that workers know their salary is not that different from anything anyone else will be able to negotiate, and that any differences are based on experience.

Productivity

In sales, it's called commission. In banking, it's called a huge Christmas bonus. The label doesn't matter, so long as the rewards are linked to productivity. One way to keep your monthly salary bill low is to link part of an employee's income to their productivity. Whether that's their individual contribution or the team's overall success is up to you. Bonuses don't have to be much, but if people know their effort will be rewarded, you're almost certainly guaranteed to get a little bit more effort from them.

Motivation

A bonus isn't the only way to motivate an employee. In fact, survey after survey has shown that remuneration isn't the main reason why people change jobs: they do it because they no longer feel valued where they work. Motivating your team doesn't necessarily have to cost you money. Sometimes a 'thank you' for a job well done is all it takes. You might think it's cheesy when you see 'Employee of the Month' certificates up on an office wall, but for that employee it really is a badge of honour. Recognition is what a lot of people work for. For others it might be the chance to take on new responsibilities or knowing that they will be in line for promotion when a position becomes available. Some people are motivated by doing something new: giving them regular challenges will keep them happy.

One of the most effective cost-free tools a manager has for motivating a team member is to explain how their work affects the team as a whole. If you don't do X by the end of the day, then Y in another department won't be able to meet the client's deadline. Which brings me on to:

Communication

The team that talks to one another is a team that can work together. That doesn't mean chatting all day and not getting any work done, it means proper communication about what needs to be done, who is doing what and when it will be completed.

It may be necessary to formalise your communication. Plenty of companies start their week with a big meeting at 9 a.m. on a Monday morning to set the agenda for the next seven days. When you have different departments or individuals contributing to a project, then making sure they update each other on their progress, or lack of it, is vital.

It's also important that people know they can turn to their boss if they feel things aren't being communicated properly. If you are in charge, make sure your team know they can contact you if they have a problem.

Oversight

If a team member knows that at the end of the week, or the project, or the year, they are going to have to sit down with their boss to discuss their work, they are likely to work harder than if they think no one is paying attention. However, it's important to remember that oversight isn't about catching people out, it's about checking that they have all the resources they need and offering help where it's required.

MISTAKE 37

Overcomplication

WHAT BUSINESS ARE YOU IN? THE BEST ANSWER IS almost always a short answer. If you can't explain what your business does – and most importantly who it's for – in a sentence, then you don't really know what your business is.

By and large, the simplest businesses are the strongest and if you overcomplicate your business you confuse your customers and make things difficult for your staff. You also risk getting muddled yourself as it's always difficult to know which project needs your time and concentration.

Get some focus

A simple business does not, however, mean a business that only does one thing: it means a business that only has one focus. Let me explain. Imagine for a moment that you're a hotelier in a resort town in Britain. Your hotel is a modest business so, following advice from someone like me, you make the effort to find new revenue streams. You realise that you could also offer a taxi service to pick guests up from the station, or after they've had dinner on the seafront. Perhaps there's a market for offering surf lessons, or hiring fishing equipment. Maybe your guests would like a picnic hamper for days out, or you could hire out your kitchen for cookery demon-strations. With a bit of effort, perhaps you identify eight additional revenue streams. Now, what business are you in?

If your answer is that you run a hotel but also operate a taxi service and offer surf lessons, plus there are a few other things on the side, then my first reaction is that you have overcomplicated your business. If, however, you told me that you were in the *holiday* business, then suddenly I – and hopefully you – would realise that you only have a single focus, which is making sure your guests have the best possible time.

At the other end of the business spectrum, inter-national oil firm BP has diversified into renewable energy in the past decade. This might seem at first to be contradictory: after all, isn't one the enemy of the other? However, such a move makes sense when you realise that BP has stopped being exclusively an oil business and started being an *energy* business. Diversification doesn't have to mean disintegration if you keep your focus.

Simple is better than confused

History tells us that when things get too complicated, they fail. The financial crash of 2008 was largely caused because banks had been trading financial instruments so compli-cated the bankers didn't understand them. Enron, the failed US energy company, started creating subsidiaries to hide the company's debt and it got so complicated that few knew where the debt had disappeared to. Woolworths, you could also argue, failed because it expanded its range of goods too far – was it a sweetshop, a record shop, a children's clothes shop, a DIY shop or a toy shop? – and then couldn't decide if it was a high-street business, an online retailer or an out-of-town superstore.

If your business has several income streams, or serves several markets, then try and find the thing that unifies them. The best way to do this is to think how you serve your customers and work out what business *they* think you're in. If you can bring the same focus to your various strands then you make your business more coherent. Crucially, you make it easier to explain to the people who you hope will buy from you.

If you can't find a unifying focus for your business, you might want to think about jettisoning part of your business. You might be able to sell it, or you could start a separate company for it. You might even be better off if you just ditch it: if you gain focus and purpose by losing it, the rest of your business stands to flourish.

Case study 7: Swissair

In the 1980s, Swissair was one of the world's most profitable and respected airlines. Like the nation whose flag it sported on its tail fins, Swissair was seen as dependable and financially robust. It was even known as 'the flying bank'. In fact, its cashflow was so good, and it had so much surplus capital, that the management consultancy firm McKinsey came up with a strategy to help them spend some of their massive profits: buy other airlines.

In the 1990s, the airline industry coalesced into a series of alliances where back-office services were shared between individual companies. In the years before online booking, this was of enormous benefit to customers who could now book multiple flights with partner airlines in one phone call rather than dealing with umpteen different carriers.

McKinsey's strategy was to take this idea to the next level and for Swissair to have an equity stake in its partner airlines. The business began with some urgency to actively look for candidates under its 'Hunter Strategy' as it was felt the time was right to capitalise on the lower valuations of aviation businesses following the first Gulf war. In rapid succession, Swissair took stakes in the Belgian national carrier, Sabena, followed by others including TAP Air Portugal, Austrian Airlines, Air Europe and South African Airways. In total, it took stakes in 15 separate companies in the space of six years between 1994 and 2000, making it one of the biggest operators in the industry.

Swissair had pretty deep pockets, but an airline is among one of the most expensive things you can do with your money, which meant many of the later deals relied heavily on leverage, i.e., debt. This would have been fine, of course, so long as the purchased companies produced revenues to cover the loans, but they didn't.

Swissair had got Sabena on the cheap because it was making a loss. If they had been able to turn Sabena around and make it profitable, then it would have looked like an extremely astute move, but increased competition from new entrant low-cost carriers like EasyJet and Ryanair made such a turnaround impossible.

By the turn of the century, Swissair was in trouble. It had massive debts and its income was being squeezed. And then, in 2001, the terrorist attacks of 9/11 sent the airline's income plummeting. It couldn't pay its debts. The Swiss government stepped in with temporary lending, but this was not enough and the business was put into liquidation in 2002.

So what was Swissair's biggest mistake? It could be argued hiring McKinsey in the first place was a pretty big mistake, as it was a way for the management to absolve themselves of responsibility for strategy. Not taking responsibility has consequences. The business would also appear to have failed to have carried out a sensitivity analysis of any worth, otherwise the risk of overleveraging would have prevented much of the Hunter Strategy being implemented. It was clearly guilty of thinking the market would never change, utterly failing to predict the arrival of low-cost carriers or the impact of a major global event on the industry. Had Swissair kept its pre-acquisition war chest, it would have had the funds to compete with its new rivals and to have withstood the climate after 9/11. But that wasn't its biggest mistake.

Growing too fast was the error that sealed its fate. If it had been less aggressive in its acquisitions, the mergers with subsidiary airlines could have been properly integrated, which would have led to massive efficiency savings, which in turn would have created profits that would have helped fund the next purchase. In my opinion, it was Swissair's astonishing rate of growth that meant it didn't have the right people in the right jobs at the right time. That *in turn meant there was inevitable duplication of service, not to mention occasional conflicts of interest. This is a classic case of where less ambition would have produced greater results.*

MISTAKE

38

Disrespecting the customer

I'VE GOT ANOTHER QUESTION FOR YOU, AND THIS ONE is really easy: who's the most important person in your company? Is it you? Your top salesperson? The PA who holds everything together? Wrong on every count. It is, of course, your customer.

Your customer IS your business

A business without customers can't exist so a business that doesn't hold its customers in the highest esteem will soon run into trouble. If the customers of designer clothes shops felt that the sales assistants were making fun of them for spending such large amounts of money on clothes they will rarely wear, then they would be unlikely to shop there. Similarly, if they thought the owners of that business saw them as mugs for spending thousands on something that cost a fraction of that to make, then they would probably take their money to somewhere they felt their taste and decision-making was admired. Equally, you can bet that the bargain hunters in Primark would think twice about shoving quite so many items into their baskets if they thought the owners and designers of the business thought they were tasteless idiots who will buy anything if the price is right. No one likes to be thought of as a fool, and if you make your customers feel like one they will soon take their revenge.

Just about the single biggest mistake in British business history was made by Gerald Ratner, the chief executive of Britain's biggest jewellery retailer, Ratners. He famously gave a speech to the prestigious Institute of Directors (IoD) in which he attempted to explain why – in the middle of a recession in 1991 – Ratners was still increasing its profits. Instead of explaining that Ratners had reduced the cost of production to make cheaper jewellery that people could still afford, he said that the reason he could offer his products so cheaply was because they were, and I quote, 'total crap'. It was a gag that got a big laugh from the members of the IoD, and when Gerald Ratner finished his speech he got a standing ovation.

Ratner thought he was making fun of himself. At worst he had made fun of his products. What he didn't realise – until the press got hold of the story and his takings went down – was that he had actually made fun of his customers. As one tabloid headline put it, he had turned them into '22-carat mugs'.

Gerald Ratner paid a very high price for his gaffe. The business's turnover was slashed overnight, the share price slumped by half and he was forced to resign. Not long after he left the company, the Ratners name was taken down from over the door of the chain's 800 shops.

If ever there was a lesson in the importance of respecting your customers, Ratners is it. And you don't have to be high profile like Ratner to suffer the consequences. Imagine if a local shopkeeper was overheard gossiping about his customers and that gossip made its way around the neighbourhood. Customers will put up with poor service and high prices if they need your goods enough, but if they think they are being treated disrespectfully, they will quickly – and permanently – find an alternative to your business.

In 2010, Facebook upset its users by changing its terms and conditions relating to privacy. Information which had previously only been shared if users opted-in was suddenly shared by default unless users opted out. While Facebook was never in danger of millions of its users quitting, many thousands did and the media started to scrutinise Facebook's policies like never before. It was hardly a Ratner moment, but it will have convinced tens of thousands of potential users to stay away. By not respecting users' privacy, they were disrespecting the users themselves. It took a while, but Facebook eventually changed their terms and conditions back as they realised it was bad for their image, and ultimately bad for business.

Another online giant, Google, also angered its customers when it launched a service in 2010 that was intended to rival Facebook: a social network it called Buzz. When customers who already had a googlemail or gmail account joined Buzz there were instant suggestions about who they could befriend on Buzz based on . . . the people they had recently sent emails to. This meant Google had been tracking – or as some would see it, spying – on their customers and compiling very personal information about whom they had been in contact with.

Google was accused of compromising individuals' privacy again in 2010 when it was revealed that while it had been photographing the streets of the world for its Street View service, it had also scanned wifi signals coming from houses and – it claimed inadvertently – discovered some properties' MAC (Media Access Control) details so they could marry up online surfing habits with real-world addresses. Sounds like Big Brother to me. Unsurprisingly, I now know a lot of people who have deleted their googlemail account and the bad publicity they received will have tarnished Google's otherwise strong reputation.

Clearly, Facebook and Google are still two of the world's largest companies, but if they or any other company disrespect their users' privacy, they create an opportunity for their own Ratner moment, and the space for a rival to flourish. If it ever happened that the names and addresses, or the direct debit details, of my members became public, I would expect thousands of them to immediately stop their membership in protest and disgust. You just can't get away with disrespecting your customers these days.

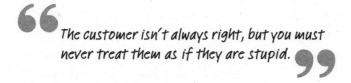

The customer isn't always right, but you must never treat them as if they are stupid.

That doesn't mean that the customer is always right – quite often they're not – but it does mean that your customer is never stupid. Customers make rational choices about who to buy from at what price; it is your job to work out which of them will buy from you at your price. And if people choose to do that, or choose not to do that, it doesn't make them stupid.

MISTAKE

39

Thinking markets will never change

YOU SET UP YOUR BUSINESS. YOU FIND A REGULAR supply of customers. You establish great relationships with your suppliers. Your revenue easily outstrips your costs. All you have to do from now on to enjoy a very nice income is maintain the status quo. Easy.

Losing touch with reality

For a few years it might well be easy, but then – so slowly it might take you years to realise it – your customers begin to tail off and your profits start a gentle slide. It doesn't matter too much because you're still in profit and your income hasn't dropped sharply enough to spur you into making changes.

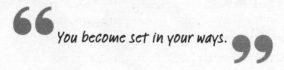

You become set in your ways.

What happens next is . . . nothing. You become set in your ways. You think you know your business and know your industry; after all, you've been doing it for decades. And then, finally, you dip into the red and you are forced to acknowledge that maybe you need to 'move with the times'. Christ, you say to yourself, the fact that I'm even saying something like 'move with the times' must mean I'm past it. Then you tell yourself that you're not going to give up without a fight. You're going to relaunch, up your game and reclaim your lost customers.

Now, one of two things may happen. Either you:

a) pick yourself up and go and hunt down your old customers and find that they have discovered a business to replace yours (and they wouldn't go back to you because they think you're so dated); or

b) your business has been so poorly run for so long that you don't have the funds in the bank to relaunch, or you're too tired and bitter to take it on.

Consequently, one way or another, your once-successful business goes down the pan.

This may sound like an exaggerated scenario, but I bet you could walk down any high street in Britain and spot a business that fits this particular bill. It might be a gentlemen's outfitters that's lucky to sell a couple of dressing gowns in the run-up to Christmas or a few tweed hats when the grouse season starts, or a bookshop that feels like a library rather than a place you can discuss the latest thriller with a mate, or a nationwide chain that never seems to stock anything you like any more. Britain's high streets are full of visible examples of businesses failing their market. And if you look up at the businesses that operate above those shops, or on industrial estates or in financial districts, you'll find businesses that are also in a terminal decline. Imagine, for example, a logistics company that hadn't let its clients track deliveries online, or a wholesaler that didn't take credit cards.

In the 1990s, one of the greatest British brands nearly hit the buffers. Marks and Spencer (M&S) had thought that there would always be a market for its dependable range of unfussy clothing, but its customers thought differently. M&S's clothes began to look dated and the fact that they didn't take credit cards other than their own expensive charge card – which seems utterly unbelievable now – meant that they were turning away customers who might otherwise have bought something. Profits slumped, the share price plummeted and the business was nearly taken over.

Within a few years, M&S had gone from being dependable to frumpy even though it had barely changed: the market moved and it didn't. Not taking payment by credit card highlights just how much they had lost touch with consumers. It wasn't a case of their designers producing the odd dud range, M&S had become so inward-looking that it failed to spot one of the biggest changes in shoppers' behaviour. While M&S customers were still writing out cheques – remember them? – at the till, its rivals' tills were ringing with speedy card transactions.

Now that M&S has made such a spectacular recovery with its increased food sales and ambitious TV ads, it's easy to forget just how tired the business had become. Sir Stuart Rose, who was brought in as the new CEO in 2004, instantly recognised that the market had moved away from the retailer and brought in new product ranges, redesigned the stores and put millions into advertising to let lapsed customers know they should give the old dinosaur another look.

Moving with the market is a key plank of any successful business strategy and it really isn't that hard. If you subscribe to the trade magazines and websites for your industry, you will pick up the trends. If you visit the trade shows and conventions for your industry you'll meet new suppliers and clients. And when you travel you'll see how similar businesses overseas compare to yours. In the case of Marks and Spencer, just taking a walk down the high street and having a look at what people were wearing would have been enough.

Make time to think about the future

The secret to staying relevant is to be organised about it, otherwise it's too easy to carry on with the way things are. You need to set aside time to sit down and think about future trends and where your market is heading. I have quarterly meetings with my top team to do a SWOT (Strengths, Weaknesses, Opportunities, Threats) analysis for my various businesses. It's always very interesting when we get to discussing the Os. One of us might have used a health club abroad and seen a new piece of equipment, another might have studied the accounts of a rival operator and found that those with spa facilities were doing better or worse than those without, or someone might have been approached by a new merchandising company who has fantastic ideas about our range of in-club goods. All these opportunities get discussed, and if we think they're worth pursuing, someone will be given the task of costing the necessary changes.

Having this meeting quarterly means we never get left behind, but for other industries it might make more sense to set aside a specific time of the year for your future-gazing. Of course, spotting an opportunity or a threat isn't enough: you have to react to it. The owners of Our Price, Woolworths, Zavvi or HMV will all tell you their business suffered because customers started downloading their music. These were all businesses with a reputation for selling music, and yet none of them started selling downloads until a company previously best known for selling desktop computers – Apple – had already become the biggest music retailer in the country. They all knew that change was coming, but they didn't do anything significant about it.

There are plenty of dates you need to have in your diary to make sure you get things like your VAT return in on time, or pay your invoices or go to a convention. You just need to make sure that you also put some time in the diary to gaze into your crystal ball. Or at least take a walk down the high street and have a look around at how your customers are behaving or what the competition is doing.

MISTAKE

40

Just not good enough

THE DELOREAN MOTOR COMPANY SHOULD NOT HAVE failed. It was led by one of the most experienced executives in the motor industry and the car's production costs were subsidised by government grants. Yet by the time the film *Back to the Future* turned the company's single model – the DMC-12 – into a time machine, John DeLorean's business had already gone bust because, well, the car just wasn't very good.

In *Dragons' Den*, Theo has got himself a reputation as a bit of a wrecker. If someone brings in a product, he will quite happily sit there for 15 minutes trying to pull it apart. If it breaks, he won't be investing and neither will the rest of us. Why? Because the product just isn't good enough.

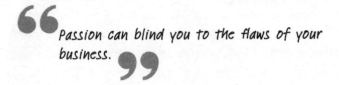

> *Passion can blind you to the flaws of your business.*

When you are starting a new business, it can be extremely tempting to launch before you are ready. You have so much passion for your product or your service that you can't wait to share it with customers. But that passion can also make you blind to your business's flaws.

The trouble is, if you don't own up to your flaws, your customers will soon tell you about them. If your product is shoddy or not fit for purpose, people will want their money back. If your service is inept or slow, customers will walk away, never to return. If your branding is unappealing, you won't attract customers. If your premises aren't ready, you'll put people off (or, worse, fall foul of health and safety legislation). If you don't have your finances in place, you could go bust if sales dip even a little or costs rise by a fraction. Let me be clear about this: if you're not ready, if your team isn't ready and if your product isn't as good as it can be, then do yourself a massive favour and delay your launch.

Businesses don't have to be terrible to fail, they just have to be less than they ought to be. One very good reason for this is that you might be giving away a valuable secret. You are giving potential rivals the idea that your business might be something for them to copy. And if their copycat business makes sure its product is perfect and its service flawless, then they are going to put you out of business before you have a chance to get going.

Being sub-standard isn't always immediately fatal for a business. Some customers are willing to lower their expectations if you slash your prices. However, a plumber who leaves his customer with a leak, a web design company that infects their customers with bugs and glitches, or a product that doesn't deliver on the promises made in its advertising will never be recommended by customers to their friends and family. Slowly but surely your customer base will shrivel and leave your business vulnerable to a slicker, hungrier rival who will take your customers from you.

MISTAKE

41

Refusing to admit you're not up to the job

ENTREPRENEURS SHARE CERTAIN CHARACTERISTICS. WE are all tenacious, by and large we are all optimistic and we all get bored easily. We are also, almost always, unbelievably stubborn. That can have its advantages, but it can also be extremely problematic. That stubborn streak means that some entrepreneurs refuse to face certain facts. Occasionally one of those facts is that they are just not up to the job and their business would be much better off with someone else at the helm.

If you've launched a business from scratch; if you've invested in it financially and emotionally; if your sense of identity and self-worth is tied up in the venture – it is really easy to understand why it's difficult to walk away. Turning round to friends, family and staff and admitting you don't have what it takes is a heartbreaking prospect, and that's why people don't do it. They carry on muddling through, making mistakes and missing opportunities.

None of us see ourselves particularly clearly. We tend to be blind to our faults and overly impressed by our own talents, but if your business isn't doing as well as you think it should be doing, you might want to look very close to home. If you realise that your business needs someone with greater experience, more financial knowledge, better people skills or sales ability, then you owe it to yourself and to the business to step aside.

> 66 Would you get an interview for your own job? 99

A good way of assessing if you are the problem is to write a job description for the CEO of your business. What tasks and roles need to be fulfilled? Then imagine you instruct a recruitment agency to hire your dream CEO. What skills would you want them to have? Now ask yourself this: would you get an interview for that job? And if not, who would you give an interview to?

You don't have to leave the company to hand over the reins to a more experienced operator. Perhaps, like me, you could employ a chief executive and take on a chairman's role. Or maybe you would be more suited to a role that played to your strengths while someone better able to lead the business takes it forward. Just imagine what you could achieve if you were freed up to concentrate on the things you do best.

Even if this sounds tempting, in reality hiring someone to take on the CEO's role – and then having to answer to them – is likely to be a complicated decision. What happens if the two of you disagree? Who would answer to whom? You would need to have a 'conflict resolution' plan in place before you took someone on. You would also need to agree in advance how the new boss would be assessed. Not having clearly defined roles and responsibilities for each of you is potentially as destructive to the business as you staying in your current position. The best and fairest way to do it is to create a board of directors for the new CEO to report to. You might be on that board, but if decisions are taken democratically, the new CEO can get on with the job without direct interference from you. It's a very tough position to put yourself in, but if it's that or losing the business, it could be a very smart decision.

There are several examples of founders realising they weren't the best CEO, and my favourite is eBay. It was started in 1995 by a computer engineer called Pierre Omidyar. Not only was he brilliant with code and computers, but he was smart enough to realise, when people started using his trading platform, that it had potential. In 1996, he met an experienced MBA graduate called Jeff Skoll and promptly hired him as the company's first President. Skoll set about writing a business plan for eBay, and when he realised just how much potential Omidyar's idea had, decided that even he didn't have the experience to take it forward. And so he used his business plan to tempt one of the most high-profile executives in corporate America, Meg Whitman, who had previously worked at Disney, Hasbro and Procter & Gamble, to turn eBay into the global giant we know today.

Pierre Omidyar's most profitable day at work was writing the online auction software itself, but his second most profitable day was when he hired Skoll. And Jeff Skoll earned all his share options and salary the day he realised the business needed someone with Whitman's skills. Needless to say, eBay is now a fantastically successful business. If you think you can't hand over your business to someone else, just take a moment to think about whether that's better than having no business at all. And also spend some time wondering if someone else could help you turn your business into the next eBay.

I find it interesting that when I meet entrepreneurs whose businesses have gone under, the reasons they give me for the failure usually relate to an external factor; perhaps a rival launched, or a new product came out, or they had problems with cashflow, or some other reason beyond their control. Hardly anyone ever says, 'I wasn't up to the job.' What they don't realise is that not anticipating a competitor coming to town, or a rival product launching, or taking action to combat cashflow issues, all actually add up to the same thing: the person in charge isn't up to the job. It takes someone special to admit that they are the problem rather than looking for something else to blame.

MISTAKE

42

Selling at the wrong time

WE'RE ALL QUITE USED TO THE FACT THAT THERE'S A GOOD time and a bad time to buy and sell property. If you're smart (or lucky) you'll buy property at the beginning of a rise in prices, and sell just before the market tanks. Or you might try and buy in an up-and-coming neighbourhood to maximise your gains. Or look for a property you can add value to. Or you might put your house on the market in late spring when your garden's looking at its best.

Of course, for you to be able to buy and sell at the right time means that someone else is doing it at the wrong time. Someone else has failed to see the potential in the up-and-coming area or the potential in the property, and sold their asset in the wrong condition or at the wrong time.

There are very similar considerations when thinking about selling a business. For starters, you have to have something that people will want to buy, and generally speaking buyers are looking to acquire one of two things: profits or assets. Some assets are easier to value than others; for instance, I'd be pretty sure of the valuation of a building and less sure of the valuation of a mailing list. The more certain a buyer is of the quality of the asset, the better its valuation. Of course, any debt your business has is taken off its valuation.

All of which means that if your business is at a very early stage where your revenues are low and your assets are little more than a website and a mailing list, there is no reason for someone to buy your business. They don't need to buy your idea when they can just copy it.

If you have profits and assets to sell, then you might make more money selling them to different buyers. There are buyers who specialise in 'asset stripping' companies and look to find businesses where the parts are potentially worth more than the whole. If you think this might apply to your business (e.g., you have a particularly good location that would be valuable to one company, and revenues that would be unaffected by a move to a cheaper location) then you should split the two before you put your business up for sale.

Timing is everything

Unlike property, where a large percentage of potential buyers just want somewhere to live and are therefore less worried about the future value of the property, in business you are not just selling existing value, you are selling the promise of *future* income. This means that timing the sale of your business makes a massive difference to the price buyers will be willing pay for it.

Take the case of two clothing retailers who both announced plans to float on the stock market in 2010. The first was New Look, a business that was 40 years old and had over 1,000 branches worldwide. The other was Superdry, the super-trendy label once favoured by David Beckham and worn by teenagers *and* their parents. The New Look sale never happened because there weren't enough brokers willing to buy the shares, whereas Superdry floated in March for £400 million and its value soared to nearly £1 billion by the end of the year.

There will be plenty of reasons why one flotation was a success and the other was over before it started, but one of them, undoubtedly, was timing. New Look was perceived by brokers as a business that had reached saturation point and probably had nowhere else to go. Superdry, on the other hand, had ambitious expansion plans and looked set to conquer high streets all over the world. Fashion is famously a fickle business, which means Superdry won't be supercool for ever. Julian Dunkerton, the brand's founder, went to the market at just the right time.

Buyers like to minimise the chances that they are about to waste their money. One way they can do this is if they can compare the valuation of your company with that of a similar business. Just as house buyers like to know they are not paying more for their house than the house down the road, business buyers are reassured by open market valuations.

If a similar business to yours has just sold for ten times its profit, then the chances are you'll find buyers willing to pay the same multiple for your business. If, alternatively, the economy or the industry takes a downturn, that multiple will come down. When a business in your industry suddenly sells for a lot of money, you might want to think about selling.

You only have to look back a few years to the dotcom bubble to see businesses that changed hands for ridiculous valuations (even when they weren't making a profit) that were next to worthless after the crash.

The dotcom revolution continues to have an impact on valuations, particularly for media companies. Now that people can get their news, cinema listings and celebrity interviews free of charge online, the revenues of newspaper groups have dropped like a stone. They have huge buildings, massive staffing levels (though not as massive as they used to be), significant printing and distribution costs and declining revenues. In a decade, the valuation of traditional media companies has been hammered.

Which explains why one of the biggest global media brands, the respected American magazine *Newsweek*, was sold in 2010 for the total sum of $1. Yup, just one measly dollar. Somebody certainly didn't know when to sell that one.

Case study 8: Royal Bank of Scotland

In the 1990s, the Royal Bank of Scotland (RBS) was one of the most respected names in British banking. In the 2000s, the company experienced a period of rapid expansion – by market capitalisation it became the fifth biggest bank in the world – which ended in a spectacular bust that led to the bank being bailed out by the government. So what went wrong?

In 1999, RBS began negotiations to buy NatWest, one of the biggest banks in Britain, even though NatWest was four times the size of RBS. A string of bad performances had meant NatWest's share price had plummeted and RBS seized its moment. It was generally considered a brilliant move by RBS and the man who got the credit for sealing the deal was a guy called Fred Goodwin who had been the bank's deputy CEO. Once he was promoted to the top job in 2001, Goodwin – emboldened by the success of the NatWest deal – began ratcheting up RBS's acquisitions.

In the six years after Goodwin took the helm, RBS's assets quadrupled and its share price soared. The bank bought Direct Line and Churchill, two of the biggest insurance companies in Britain, as well as other banks in Europe, China and the US. At the same time, it ramped up its lending to the corporate sector, providing the funds for several leveraged buyouts. All this meant that RBS went from being fully funded – i.e., its lending and acquisitions were funded by money it held for depositors – to being reliant on the wholesale banking market.

We now know that so-called Collateralised Debt Obligations (CDOs), the new banking product that led to a boom in lending, were building up risk in the banking sector. But in the early years of the 21st century, many people in banking believed that CDOs had virtually eliminated debt by packaging up slices of high-risk and low-risk debt into bonds; it was thought that if one debt went bad, the holders of the bonds would hardly notice. In 2007, however, people did start to notice and we all became familiar with the term 'credit crunch'. The US housing market plummeted, home owners defaulted on their mortgages and the debt that had been spread out via CDOs infected the entire banking system with panic.

Fred Goodwin, bolstered by his bank's recent performance, felt RBS was immune from the CDO virus and went ahead with the purchase of part of a Dutch bank, ABN Amro, at a cost of approximately £10 billion. Just a few months later, however, ABN Amro would have cost a lot less after it became clear that it had a massive exposure to the US housing market.

RBS, the powerhouse of British banking, rapidly unravelled. Its clients started to default on their loans; the wholesale market dried up in the CDO panic; its income nosedived and its share price crashed (at one point it was at just 2 per cent of its 2007 peak). Had it not been for a government bailout, RBS would have gone bust.

Goodwin received much of the blame for the downfall of RBS, and even though he resigned immediately after the bailout, the fact that he got a pay-off and kept the bulk of his pension entitlement caused widespread anger. Goodwin made many mistakes, and his perceived arrogance certainly didn't help his cause. But his biggest mistake was the timing of the ABN purchase. Just as there is a right time to sell an asset, there is a wrong time to buy it and Goodwin timed the deal spectacularly badly. If he had not been so impatient, RBS might just have weathered the financial storm intact.

MISTAKE

43

The biggest mistake in business...

I'VE SAVED THE BIGGEST MISTAKE IN BUSINESS TILL LAST.
And not only is it the biggest mistake, it is – by far – the most
common mistake. It is not doing it at all.

I lost count a very long time ago of the people who have
told me they had a brilliant idea for a business, but just didn't
have the time. Or the money. Or the skills. Or the experience.
Or the courage. They might think these are valid reasons for
not following their dream, but I just think they are excuses.

> **It's the things you don't do in life that you
> regret.**

It's the things you don't do in life that you regret, and if you're OK with getting five years into the future and wondering what might have been, then don't do it. But if you think you could build a business you could be proud of, make a difference and make some money, you are going to have serious regrets in five years' time and perhaps for much longer.

Even if you avoid making all the mistakes in this book, there's a chance that your business still might not be a success. You might lose a bit of money. You'll definitely lose some sleep. But I can guarantee you that – whatever the fate of your business – you will learn things about yourself, about your industry and about business that will either make you more valuable to a future employer or a better entrepreneur when you start your second business. I won't tell you that you have nothing to lose, but it's a lot less than you think when the rewards are enormous.

Working for yourself, creating a company that makes its customers happy and nurtures its staff is one of the most remarkable journeys you can go on. So ask yourself this: isn't it time you took your first step? And if not now, when? If you don't do it, somebody else will. If that happens, you will kick yourself so hard the bruise will never go away.

So, really, what are you waiting for?

Index

valuations (business) 138–41
   accurate 140–41
   overvaluing 138–40
value added tax (VAT)
   99–100, 107
VAT (value added tax)
   99–100, 107

wages *see* salaries
Whitman, Meg 203–4
Woolworths 89, 154–5, 184,
   197

YouDoo Doll 20

Zavvi 197